THE EIGHT CONCEPTS

OF BOWEN THEORY

by

Roberta M. Gilbert M.D.

*A New Way of Thinking About
The Individual and the Group*

Leading Systems Press
Falls Church & Basye, Virginia

For additional copies of this book
and to inquire about quantity discounts,
contact:

Business Manager
Leading Systems Press
Center for the Study of Human Systems
313 Park Avenue, Suite 308
Falls Church VA 22046
or call 703 532-3823

See also www.hsystems.org .

Table of Contents

Other Books by Roberta M. Gilbert, M.D.

Extraordinary Relationships: A New Way of Thinking About Human Interactions

Turn any relationship into an extraordinary one. After food, water, and shelter, relationships are the most important factor in determining our quality of life. At work, productivity and efficiency depend on relationships. At home, relationships with our spouses, children, and friends are keys to success and happiness. This invaluable guide shows that only by further developing yourself can you further develop your relationships. Based on the innovative family systems theory pioneered by the late Dr. Murray Bowen, *Extraordinary Relationships* offers practical advice that has helped thousands of people throughout the last three decades. It's a blueprint to better relationships that tells how the principles of family systems theory can be used in all arenas of your life.

ISBN 0-471-34690-x

Connecting With Our Children: Guiding Principles for Parents in a Troubled World

Parents want a special relationship with their children. Parents care. They want to guide their children through the rough spots in life and help them make the right decisions. Research shows that parental connection is extremely important in safeguarding children against dangers such as substance abuse, sexual promiscuity, criminal activity, and suicide. This is more important than ever today. But, what does making this connection mean? *Connecting With Our Children* shows parents how to build the connection found in better relationships.

ISBN 0-471-34786-8

This book is dedicated to all those
who have learned Bowen theory,
made it a part of their lives
and are speaking, writing,
and training others
in centers
here and abroad.

INTRODUCTION

"The early family researchers of the 1954-1956 period were describing a completely new order of observations never previously described in the literature. I think it was related to the ability to finally shift thinking from an individual to a family frame of reference. . . . In my research the change came as a sudden insight shortly after schizophrenic patients and their entire families were living together on the research ward. Then it was possible to really see the family phenomenon for the first time. After it was possible to see this phenomenon in schizophrenia, it was then automatic to see varying degrees of the same thing in all people."

Murray Bowen, 1976[1]

Bowen family systems theory was developed by Dr. Murray Bowen, a psychiatrist and professor of psychiatry. He began that process in the 1940's at the Menninger Clinic, continued on at the National Institutes of Health and then at Georgetown University. His goal was to bring the study of the human into the realm of accepted science. By the time he died in 1990 he left us a new way of seeing and thinking about the human phenomenon.

A superior life course, according to this theory, is based on thinking rather than feelings, which come and go. The human's best thinking, according to this theory, is based on fact, not feeling, though feelings are given a great deal of attention. The theory is based on the family as the emotional unit, not the individual, though the individual is most important to the theory. Further, it is based on observation rather than on what people think, feel or say about themselves and others.

"Thinking systems," for most people, is a very different way of thinking. The brain must be literally retrained. Rather than thinking "cause and effect," so automatic to most of us (both by nature and by education), one looks for the interrelations of the group. Rather than noticing only how the individual is impinged, one tries always for a bigger picture. Systems thinking strives to look at the emotional process going on among people, while never losing sight of the facts of a given situation. Rather than trying for control or blaming the other, one tries always to better manage oneself and one's own contribution to the situation.

In this new way of thinking, no one is to blame or at fault. Rather, the emotional system itself operates as a unit, each one affecting all the other members. In thinking systems, one is aware of being a small part of something much larger than self – one's family in all of its generations.

Because the human family is, emotionally, a family of mammals – a natural system – the term "thinking systems" refers to natural systems, not mathematical systems. It grows out of *actual* observations of natural systems. Natural systems do not always follow the laws of mathematics.

Thinking systems also refers to watching for the emotional or automatic processes in play in a given situation of a system of people. These processes are the ones, so useful to continuing life, that can become difficult for the individual and for the system to manage. And, until Bowen theory came along, most people had little or no idea about how to think about those automatic emotional processes of groups, so powerful in all our lives.

Bowen theory is formally made up of eight remarkably cohesive concepts that deal with the human family and also with the individual.

I have learned that many people who study Bowen theory, sometimes for years, even leaders in the field, are not clear about those formal eight concepts. When asked, without notice, to list them on paper, many cannot. And though there is more to Bowen theory than these eight concepts, (or is there?) there is much to be said for getting them down pat. They are the beginning, the *sine qua non*, the foundation on which the serious student will build.

To my way of thinking, seven of the eight concepts derive in a logical progression from that most foundational concept, *the family as the emotional unit.* This book is built on that understanding, for it is as we see all the ideas in that context, that they are most easily understood and each is seen to be necessary. Here, the ideas build, from simplest to most complex, step by step. That process, because of its reasonableness, facilitates remembering the concepts.

Most of my experience with organizations has been gained in leadership seminars with clergy. For that reason, clergy and congregations are often used in examples. But they apply as well to a group in any organizational setting since human groups are predictable.

One of my favorite sayings has become: "If you know theory you can use it. If you don't you can't." Often, when faced with a relationship difficulty, I run down the list of the eight concepts, to see which applies and how. By the time I am finished I have several directives to show the way out of my difficulty. The concepts hold that kind of magic for those who understand and use them.

The eight concepts of Bowen theory, in the logical progression that builds on the family as the emotional unit, are:

- Nuclear Family Emotional System
- The Differentiation of Self Scale
- Triangles
- Cutoff
- Family Projection Process
- Multigenerational Transmission Process
- Sibling Position
- Societal Emotional Process.

Now, let us consider each in some detail, and in a way that will show their connection.

Roberta Gilbert
Basye, Virginia

NOTES

[1]Bowen, M. "Family Therapy in Clinical Practice" Jason Aronson, Northvale, NJ 1978, 1983, 1985 p. 394.

NUCLEAR FAMILY EMOTIONAL SYSTEM

The Nuclear Family is the Emotional Unit

"In the commitment of each to the other in the marriage, the two. . . fuse into a new emotional oneness. The mechanisms they use in dealing with the emotional fusion, which becomes a kind of life style for them, help to determine the kinds of problems they will encounter in the future.

"There is a spectrum of ways spouses deal with fusion symptoms. The most universal mechanism is emotional distance from each other. . . Other than the emotional distance, . . . there are three major areas. . . marital conflict; sickness or dysfunction in one spouse; and projection of the problems to children." [1]

Murray Bowen, 1971 and 1976

In Bowen family systems theory, the nuclear family, rather than the individual, is the emotional unit. This concept changes the way one thinks about everything relational, and perhaps the way one thinks about everything! This may sound startling, but it is not an overstatement. The idea leads to an entirely different, and for most, a new way of thinking – "systems thinking."

Further, upon this concept all the others are built. [2]

What does it mean to say that the family is an emotional unit? It means many things, but two are primary.

1. Whatever affects one affects each one in the system. That is, anxiety moves easily from person to person in the group.

2. Family members trade "self" into the family relationship togetherness in a family "fusion" of selves.

In Natural Systems

Let us see what it means to be an emotional unit in its most basic form; for example, my grandfather's herd of cattle. Say the cattle are peacefully grazing in the pasture. But if one cow gets too close to the electric fence, sustaining a shock, she may jump, vocalize and even jump or run, showing that she is in a very anxious state. How long does it take for the other cows in the pasture to "catch" the anxiety? Of course, it happens almost immediately. Their behavior soon becomes agitated, showing they have taken on the anxiety of the initial individual. The cattle are showing, by *the movement of anxiety* through the herd, that they are an emotional system. Anxiety that affects one, affects all.

Some important principles of Bowen theory are illustrated in this simple example:

1. Anxiety is important in emotional systems. It is usually not necessary, for the purpose of thinking systems, to describe the coloration of the anxiety (depression, elation, anger, etc.). At base, most intense emotion is simply, and can be referred to

as, anxiety. Emotions are automatic physiologic reactions. When they become conscious, they are feelings. Anxiety is automatic and most of it is out of awareness.

2. Anxiety travels in a group between and among individuals. It is infectious.

3. Where the anxiety travels defines the limits of the emotional system. A herd across the road, for example, may be watching all this excitement with interest and even get a little edgy, but it will not express nearly the degree of anxiety of the initial herd. It is a different emotional system.

Since anxiety is so important to an understanding of emotional systems, from cows to humans, let us take a little closer look at it.

Anxiety

There are two types of anxiety, acute and chronic. Acute anxiety occurs in the human on a daily basis. Examples are the reactions we get to stressors such as a fender-benders, stock market swings, or threats to the workplace. Chronic anxiety is more of a background level of anxiety that we carry with us. Much of this type of anxiety is programmed into us during our years in our family of origin, a level of anxiety that was/is usual for the family. We carry it around like a bad habit – it is more or less automatic.

Acute Anxiety

Subjected to a stressor or stressors, mammals react in predictable ways. As soon as danger is perceived, adrenalin or epinephrine is secreted from the medulla (inner cells) of the adrenal gland, (about the size of a large lima bean, sitting atop the kidney – thus ad-renal or epi-nephine.) The hormone epinephrine increases the heartbeat, the blood pressure, sweating and gives the urge to flee, fight or freeze in place. (Interestingly, some species under stress will begin to caretake.) So, the adrenalin, or acute anxiety response makes it possible for the organism to react appropriately to imminent danger.

Chronic Anxiety

If the anxiety continues, as it does with the "background" level we all carry around with us, acquired from our years of experience in our original families and/or from the circuiting of anxiety in our present family, a different set of hormones is secreted. This time the outer cells of the adrenal gland, or "cortex" are involved, secreting the cortical steroid hormones such as cortisol. Those hormones (there are several) have so many effects that we are probably just beginning to understand a few of them. They also set into motion "cascades" of other hormonal secretions and effects in literally hundreds of interactions. Among others, effects of the cortical steroids are thus anti-allergic and anti-inflammatory. They may represent the body's attempt to heal continuing cellular damage from the many effects of the chronic anxiety. They also have unwanted, "side" effects, though. Some of these include weight gain, susceptibility to infection, ulcer, and some investigators think, aging effects on the brain (that may lead to dementias).

Anxiety is Additive

Anxiety, whatever its trigger, is additive. If, in addition to that background level of anxiety one carries around from one's family, some business reverses occur, then the IRS finds a problem with one's tax return, and then a national crisis such as 9/11 happens, one's anxiety will escalate to a level much higher than usual. No matter what the trigger, the reaction is the same – anxiety. The more triggers, the higher the anxiety level rises.

The triggers may be negative, such as those listed above, or they may simply be changes. Even positive changes, such as marriage or promotion, are often reacted to physiologically with what we call the "stress response."

The Togetherness Fusions

No matter how we may try to deny it, or cut off from it, that larger organization, the family, determines a great deal about us, both our weaknesses and our strengths. To that family as well as our reactions to it and principles learned there, we are indebted for much that is good or great about ourselves. On the other hand, the same forces went into creating the patterns we wish were different, those that get us into trouble.

Much of human existence is dictated by the strong "togetherness" force originating in that most basic of social organizations, the family. That force, opposite from the "individuality force," automatically and instinctually pulls us together in a family and, emotionally defines what that family is. It sticks us together, absorbing part of each self, demanding we be there for the group. Togetherness is the force that tries to pull one back to the group when one is being "too much" a self. It says, "Be like us," "Be for us more than for yourself," or "Think as we think." It can feel so good. And it can feel so bad. It can be protective. Or it can prevent our becoming the best we can be.

In that way, that organism, so much bigger than self, of which we are all a part, the family, is made up of "donations" of self from its members – parts of selves that are there more for the family than for the individual. In that way, the members "fuse" together, or "lose self" into the family in automatic reactions that are as old as time itself. This "huddling together" or herding instinct kicks in whenever anxiety increases. To greater and lesser extents in different families, when one gets upset, all do, just like the cows. (Figure 1: By convention, males are recorded as squares and females as circles.)

As the individuals give up a part of self, these portions of self become "fused" together in a group self. All the individual is left with, to be for self, is the portion that was not fused into the group. This remaining part distinguishes each as an individual self. That amount will vary in different families, and even among different individuals in the same family.

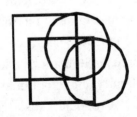

Figure 1 Family Fusions

Family Relationship Patterns

When a family member becomes stressed, just like the cows, everyone feels anxious. And the tendencies toward fusions (herding instinct) become more pronounced. The fusions, while they solve the problem of being alone and in danger, are themselves uncomfortable, adding to the anxiety. So family members may try to resolve their anxious feelings by adopting certain well-known postures toward each other. These postures, then, are actual evidence of relationship fusions, or loss of self into the group (stuck-togetherness). Togetherness (or fusion) in relationships, though an attempt to resolve anxiety, actually creates anxiety of its own, thus adding to the overall difficulty. These postures are well-known and actually look very much like the behavior of other species when in danger (fight, flight, freeze and care-take).

These postures are neither good nor bad. They are automatic and familiar to all of us because we use them so often, perhaps on a daily basis. We do not necessarily recognize when we slip into them. They are emotional, reactive responses. They do not become a problem if used briefly and if rotated in their use, as most of us do frequently. They become problematic when one of them becomes the only outlet for anxiety and repetitive to the point where no one knows how to get out of it.

The four typical patterns, or postures, that anxiety in relationships takes are:

- Triangling (or focused child).

- Conflict

- Distance
- Overfunctioning/underfunctioning reciprocity (or dysfunctional spouse)

Triangling

When a family becomes anxious, one of the automatic postures is that of the triangle, or focused child. Let's take a look at it.

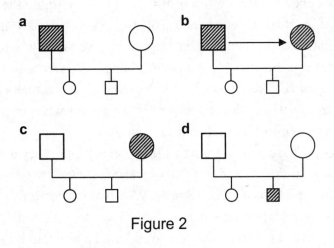

Figure 2

If one of two partners, say, the dad, comes home anxious after a very bad day (Figure 2a), how long does it take the mom to figure it out? Like the cows, she knows immediately. And, like them, she probably takes it on herself (remember how quickly it spread in the cows). He transmits (Figure 2b), and she takes on the anxiety instantly. Interestingly, as soon as she takes on the anxiety, he often calms down (Figure 2c). Now, if one of the small children comes around Mom, he or she will take it on and the anxiety will end up in the child (Figure 2d). Mom feels better. So now we have two calm parents, but an upset child. If this particular cycle happens often enough, with the anxiety ending up in the child, we have a triangle pattern.

Further, if the family anxiety tends to settle in a child long and often enough, the child will develop a *symptom* (either physical, mental/emotional, or social). The onset of the symptom will add to the parents' anxiety. They will begin to worry about the child. The more they worry, the more anxious the child becomes, intensifying the symptom, and so a vicious cycle ensues. It's easy to see why this pattern is also called the "child focus." (Figure 3).

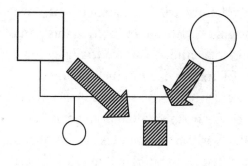

Figure 3

Triangles are so important to the human phenomenon that we find them represented in no less than five concepts of Bowen theory, in different iterations of how they play out. Since this important idea is represented as one of the eight concepts, it will be considered in more detail later.

There are many triangles in any family. It can be extremely useful to sit down and draw them out.

As we just saw, when someone takes on most of the anxiety, that individual will eventually develop symptoms. These symptoms draw more anxious focus, leading to an increase in focus, and so on and on.

Bowen said, *"There are two main variables that govern the intensity of this process in the nuclear family. The first is the degree of emotional isolation, or cutoff, from the extended family, or from others important in the relationship system. . .The second. . .has to do with the level of anxiety. . .Any. . .symptoms in the nuclear family. . .are less intense when anxiety is low and more intense when the anxiety is high."* [3]

In the family, triangled anxiety often results in a sick child. (Originally, Bowen referred to this part of theory as "projection to a child.") But the triangles can go outside the family in affairs. Also, a troubled family can triangle in many agencies such as those in the legal system or the healthcare system, in an attempt to get relief.

In the workplace, triangles always abound, as they do in a family. They can build and interlock. Leaders can become the focused one in an organization just because the leader of a group stands alone.

Internationally, triangles abound also. Reading the news any day shows the positioning and aligning of nations in many triangles in the world community. Foreign aid can create triangles – whenever aid is given, automatically enemies are created for the donor who is seen by the donee's enemies as against them. Countries often seem to get "triangled in" into difficult situations by their leaders.

Conflict

Conflict results when "*. . .neither gives in to the other on major issues. These marriages are intense in terms of the amount of emotional energy each invests in the other.*"[4]

It can become extremely bitter. These relationships carry a great deal of pain. In their struggle, they hurl accusations, each in turn, at the other. The favorite, and overused word, is "you." Projection of blame is the order of the day. Two people turn against each other in intense confrontational disagreement, competition or criticism. (Figure 4)

Figure 4   Conflict

In its extreme form in the family conflict can deteriorate into physical violence between the adults or toward the children. In the workplace conflict can drain off a great deal of energy, interfering with getting the work accomplished. In congregations conflict can mean that people become absorbed in besting each other, so that the group neglects its mission. Internationally, conflict can escalate into war, its most regrettable form. In today's world, war, of course, carries with it the ever-present danger that use of enormously destructive weapons would result in massive damage and loss of life.

Distance

Tiring of conflict, people usually turn to another automatic pattern – distance. Now, they believe, they have solved the problem. At least the conflict is over for awhile. But in reality they have solved nothing. They have merely traded one pattern for another. All the relationship postures distance people from a one-to-one relationship but sometimes the distance is so striking it actually becomes the major pattern. As Bowen said, *"The most universal mechanism is emotional distance from each other. It is present in all marriages to some degree and in a high percentage of marriages to a major degree."*[5]

Figure 5   Distance

The small lines representing emotional intensity shown in diagrams of the distance pattern are important – they explain the origin of and necessity for the distance. (Figure 5) Communications decrease and may stop. Partners may not speak to each other for months. Externally, they seem disconnected. Internally, however it is a different story. Distanced persons think about each other, the relationship and the conflict that led to it, a great deal. By distancing, they are far from free of the problem. They are still emotionally bound and defined by it.

Distanced postures can lead to separation or divorce. In the workplace a distancing posture can interfere with communications, reducing efficiency tremendously and increasing the anxiety there. Internationally, distancing is often seen. For example, though some countries "speak" a lot with each other, through their officials – others have hardly any contact at all. Trade or diplomatic sanctions of various types enact and codify the drama.

The concept of distance appears in its extreme form, as cutoff, in that important concept. (Chapter 4)

Overfunctioning/Underfunctioning Reciprocity

Originally named "dysfunction in one spouse," the overfunctioning/underfunctioning reciprocity describes partners trying to make one self out of two.[6] Bowen described it as follows: *"One spouse becomes the more dominant decision-maker for the common self, while the other adapts to the situation. This is one of the best examples of borrowing and trading of self in a close relationship. One may assume the dominant role and force the other to be adaptive. . .The dominant one gains self at the expense of the more adaptive one, who loses self.[7]*

"Each does some adapting to the other and it is usual for each to believe that he or she gives in more than the other. The one who functions for long periods of time in the adaptive position gradually loses the ability to function and make decisions for self. At that point, it requires no more than a moderate increase in stress to trigger the adaptive one into dysfunction, which can be physical illness, emotional illness or social illness, such as drinking, acting out and irresponsible behavior."[8]

17

This relationship pattern is somewhat of a see-saw. As one does well, the other falters more.

The overfunctioner:

- Knows the answers

- Does well in life

- Tells the other what to do, how to think, how to feel

- Tries to help too much

- Assumes increasing responsibility for the other

- Does things for the other he or she could do for self

- Sees the other as "the problem"

- Demands agreement, bringing on "groupthink"

The underfunctioner:

- Relies on the other to know what to do

- Asks for advice unnecessarily

- Takes all offered help, needed or not, becoming passive

- Asks the other to do what he or she can do for self

- Sees self as "the problem"

- Is susceptible to "groupthink"

- Eventually becomes symptomatic

- Gives in on everything

In the family those involved in an overfunction-ing/underfunctioning relationship may spend a great deal of time seeking and getting more and more help for the under-functioner's symptoms. The more one tries to help, the more the other goes downhill (Figure 6).

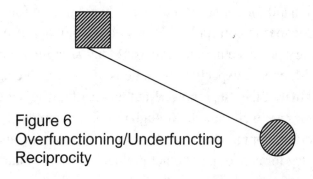

Figure 6
Overfunctioning/Underfuncting
Reciprocity

In the workplace, leaders can be overfunctioners. If that happens we will see an ebbing of the energy and pro-ductivity of the group. They can also be underfunctioners, not really being involved or doing their job. Here, the others will eventually go off on tangents.

In congregations, clergy may inherit a group that is used to being "done for," expecting him or her to do all the work while they sit back and watch or criticize. Or, clergy may go into a leadership underfunction, and watch while others appear as leaders or see the congregation go into a frenzy of activity that may or may not fit with the mission of the group. If it is a highly responsible and active group, it may organize and motivate itself, making the leader irrelevant. More often, an underfunctioning leader wreaks chaos in an organization. Important decisions do not get made and creative ideas get squelched or not followed up on.

An overfunctioner at work can be an underfunctioner at home and vice versa, depending on how the relationship patterns form.

International examples of overfunctioning include foreign aid for countries that really do not need it (or when it only goes to corrupt leaders anyway), maintaining a military presence in other countries long after the need for one is gone, or expecting the nations of the world to agree with that of the "superpower" automatically, whether the policies are well thought through or not. Examples of underfunctioning internationally would be blaming another country for economic or other problems or demanding and getting financial aid when there would be a better way to put the country on a sound economic basis (not focusing on what the country can do to better itself but expecting others to do this job for them). All of this would appear, often to be the result of low level leadership – leaders operating out of emotions or automatic responses rather than out of thought-through principles.

About the Relationship Patterns

By knowing about the patterns we are able, at times, to watch for and see anxiety traveling in a system. When the anxiety is intense, the patterns are more visible. When the anxiety is low, there may be few or no apparent patterns at all.

Relationship Fusions

Looking at the family as a nuclear unit that is joined together partly by its need to manage anxiety, it becomes clear that, as anxiety increases, an intense togetherness can click into place. More togetherness means that individuals lose self to the group and that anxiety flows more quickly between them – the definition of relationship *fusions*. The fusions add to the anxiety, which people then try to handle by means of the relationship postures. We have seen that the postures or patterns also add to the anxiety. So togetherness, as a way of managing anxiety, while it is automatic (a part of the emotional system) and may work well for other species, for the human, togetherness is more of a problem than a solution.

Anxiety in Relationships

After anxiety reaches a certain level (different for each person), it overpowers thoughtful response. Logic is unavailable. It is as if the cerebral cortex (the thinking part of the brain) is "flooded" with anxiety. When that happens the cerebrum is unable to function properly.[9] Without the ability to be logical or give a thoughtful response, a relationship snag cannot be resolved. So, the anxiety continues to escalate. As anxiety escalates, the relationship postures snap into place. The patterns then contribute more anxiety to an already overloaded situation.

The Emotional System in Organizations

Are organizations emotional systems also? It appears to be the case. Theoretically, all that is necessary to create an emotional system is *spending time together*. If people spend enough time together they begin to form an emotional system similar to that of the family. Indeed, sometimes people spend more time in their organizations than in their families. The same patterns can be observed in organizations and the same principles that govern emotional processes in families apply.

Anxiety, beyond a certain level, disrupts the functioning of a group and reduces its working efficiency. In extreme cases it can destroy functioning altogether and, even the organization itself.

On the other hand, anxiety can be managed within an individual who can thereby interrupt its circuiting around the system. It will then go to a more tolerable level, allowing working efficiency and teamwork to reappear.

Interrupting the Patterns

Caught in escalating anxiety, with all its potential pitfalls, how does one think about reversing the cycle? How does one make a difference?

On reflection, one can easily see that if any of the people caught in the relationship patterns were to manage their own part of the relationship differently, the pattern would disappear. My grandfather's task, herding the cows on the way back to the barn, was, to be a very "calm presence." He would sing and talk softly to them, knowing that upset cows give very little milk.

About conflict, our grandmothers were right – it really does take two to make a fight. If only one of the parties steps back, takes a deep breath and calms down, "a soft answer turneth away wrath."

In the distance pattern, there is always a way to begin to make contact with the other – to connect. It may not be verbally at first, it may be through a gesture, or simply a different attitude. But, a connection can be made and it takes only one being more responsible in the relationship to begin the process.

Both the overfunctioner and the underfunctioner can strive for more of an equal posture. The overfunctioner can stop knowing all the answers, or not talk more than he/she listens, or not help where help is not needed. The underfunctioner's effort, on the other hand, will be to be more of a self to the other – start to think of his/her own answers, enter into the conversation more and start to do for self.

The triangler has choices, too. By understanding that one is displacing anxiety to a third, one can begin to work on self in original one-to-one relationship. If when one comes home from work spewing anxiety, as described earlier in this chapter, the other, "thinking systems" can realize he/she has the option of not taking it on, or of taking it on less than usual. By staying connected with one's spouse from this calmer position, the spouse will begin to calm down. In this way, anxiety is not moved to another member of the family. Of course the anxious one also has the option of processing his or her own anxiety and not spewing it in the first place.

In any of the patterns, if one can see the anxiety behind the pattern, relating to it calmly, the pattern itself will be less an issue.

In Coaching

In the coaching situation, with anxious relationship dilemmas (often having been in an intense "tell your feelings" situation in other therapies), the coach has two invaluable opportunities to be of use. They are:

1. The coach's calm presence and

2. Bringing family systems theory to the dilemma being presented.

They cannot be overstressed. Coaching from the point of view of Bowen theory sees the defeating nature of the emotional process families are involved in. It also sees the uselessness of continued venting. If the family can begin to calm the intense process, they can begin to think their way through to solutions. The therapist's calm presence is paramount in this since calm and optimism are catching also. For the therapist, the clinical situation is one more chance to work on staying outside an emotional field.

As the coach brings ideas of Bowen theory to bear on presented situations, not only are they useful for the present, but over time, people, seeing their usefulness, adopt them as their own. As people, seeing themselves and their relationship systems through the lens of theory, work on themselves in their important systems, they are able to actually improve their functioning.

As the therapist insists that each person work on self and self only, (though the other may listen if they come to sessions together) they gradually begin to learn about separating out a little self from the fusion they have created. The therapist lays down guidelines for the session that respect boundaries for each. They are asked not to interrupt, criticize, or tell each other what to do. In this way, they learn about shoring up boundaries over time.

As theory is emphasized, people learn its basics and begin to use it on their own in real life. This means that if people take theory seriously, they will be working on getting out of their fusions and patterns, relatively speaking. As they do that, relationships begin to work better.

Leaders and Parents

Parents, the leaders of the nuclear family, are a wonderful paradigm for leaders. As parents and leaders begin to observe the movement of anxiety within their systems, taking less of it on, and broadcasting less to others, the system is relieved of a great load. As they better understand fusions, and their resultant patterns, they can also see gradual steps to take to lessen them. The relationships in such a system begin to operate more cooperatively, beginning with those between the parents themselves, or among the leaders at the top of an organization. If those relationships improve, relationships in the entire family/organization improve. As that happens, there are less symptoms and the family or organization is freer to be the best it can be.

NOTES

[1] Bowen, M "Family Therapy in Clinical Practice" Aronson, New York, 1978, 1983, 1985 pp 203, 377.

[2] Thinking systems contrasts with existing theory in some important ways. One of these is where the focus is. Traditionally, the individual has been the focus of study – how the person gets sick, what causes the

individual to become anxious, depressed or angry, and how the individual deals with these phenomena. In thinking systems, the focus is on the *whole* relationship system, how emotions circulate through it and the different processes or patterns that arise automatically in the process.

[3] Ibid p. 379.

[4] Ibid p.204.

[5] Ibid p.377.

[6] Papero, D "Bowen Family Systems Theory" Allyn and Bacon, Boston, 1990 p.51.

[7] Bowen, Op cit p. 377.

[8] Ibid p. 379.

[9] Gottmann J "The Marriage Clinic" Norton, New York, 1999 p.73.

2

THE DIFFERENTIATION OF SELF SCALE

"This scale is an effort to classify all levels of human functioning, from the lowest possible levels to the highest potential level, on a single dimension. . .It has nothing to do with emotional health or illness or pathology. There are people low on the scale who keep their lives in emotional equilibrium without. . .symptoms, and there are some higher on the scale who develop symptoms under severe stress. However, lower scale people are more vulnerable to stress. . .The scale has no correlation with intelligence or socioeconomic levels. . .The greater the degree of undifferentiation (no-self), the greater the emotional fusion into a common self with others (undifferentiated ego mass). Fusion occurs in the context of a personal or shared relationship with others and it reaches its greatest intensity in the emotional interdependency of a marriage"[1]

Murray Bowen 1972

Togetherness and Individuality, Differentiation and Undifferentiation

We have seen how the family togetherness force creates fusions in the relationships that mean we trade self and pass anxiety in the group. We saw how those relationship patterns or postures are symptoms of that fusion or togetherness.

Now let's look at a different and opposite force – the individuality force – present in all individuals. This force says, "Be yourself, be an individual. Don't be so glommed into the group. Be the best you can be!" It encourages a part of us that is uniquely human. One might call it the emotionally mature part of a person. It takes part in relationships, but not by the giving up or taking on of self. In relationships this part of self communicates and defines self to others, cooperates or not, all directed by its principles. It pushes us to be, in Bowen theory terms, a more differentiated self.

Though some researchers see evidence for differentiation (at least, variation) in other species, it is not developed in other species to anywhere near the degree that it is in the human.[2]

Of all the eight concepts of Bowen theory, seven are concerned with describing the characteristics of the family, or the group. The scale of differentiation of self is the only one that considers in depth those of the individual. It is fundamental to grasp this concept in as complete a way as possible if we are ever to engage with the important effort that it implies. That work *is to differentiate self from one's emotional systems* – the work that makes the difference in lives.

But even this concept – the one about the individual – is derived from that basic idea of the family as the emotional unit. *The degree of individuality each has depends on how fused we were/are in our family relationships.* And there is a great deal of variability among individuals, even in the same family, in that differentiation (individuality)/undifferentiation (togetherness) balance.

There had been an idea about "emotional maturity" before the concept of differentiation of self was developed. But it was different in some significant ways. First, the idea of emotional maturity did not include physical health. The concept of differentiation of self, however, includes all of life adaptation, including physical health, so that in general, the higher one is on the scale, the better physical health (as well as social and emotional adaptation).

Secondly, in the old (individual) way of thinking, emotional maturity was more or less fixed by age. After a certain age, it was thought that people were unable to change enough to benefit by psychotherapy. The scale of differentiation of self, however, stands as a challenge for all ages, prodding and demonstrating what better functioning would look like at any time in life.

It is apparent by now that many ideas are included in the concept of differentiation of self. None of the ideas is, by itself, all that difficult to understand. But keeping all of them in mind at once can be a bit of a workout.

The Differentiation of Self Scale

Humans, and to a degree, other species as well, vary in their ability to adapt to all that life brings. This variation can be described as a hypothetical scale. (Figure 7) At the lower end of the scale, people are more emotionally fused into their relationships. They also show evidence of another type of fusion – between their emotional (automatic) and intellectual functioning. That emotional/intellectual fusion may derive from the relationship fusions one grew up in. One way that may operate is that, the more we operate in relationship fusions, the greater the anxiety load affecting intellectual functioning.

At the higher end of the scale, people give up less of themselves into relationships (less relationship fusion). They also have more ability to separate their emotional and their intellectual functioning. They have more ability to separate thinking from feeling, and to choose which will predominate at a given time.

Emotionally, we are more like than different from other species. Intellectually, we are different from other species because of the greater size of the cerebral cortex of the human brain.

The scale theoretically ranks people on a spectrum between zero, the lowest possible level of differentiation and one hundred, the highest potential level.[3] Both of these points are merely hypothetical – no one is that well off or that badly off. People actually live at points in between those two. Most of the population scatters below 30. If one ever met a 50, it would be unusual. A 75 would come along only once in several hundred years.

Lowest Levels

At the lowest levels, there is more ambient anxiety within people, leading to more life problems, poorer decisions and more relationship trouble. Lower level people are more fused into relationships. That is, they give up (lose) and take on (gain) more of self in relationships. These fusions in relationships are what give rise to the patterns and postures described in the last chapter. By itself, fusion gives rise to anxiety. While fusion solves togetherness "needs" – an innate push within the individual to unite with another – it is an effort to make a common self out of two[4] and gives rise to anxiety. It is uncomfortable to give up part of oneself or, for that matter, take on part of someone else's. This discomfort is part of their ambient anxiety.

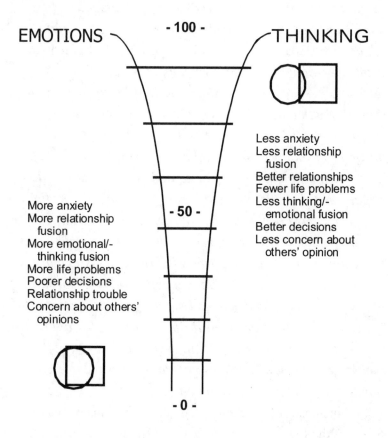

Figure 7 Scale of Differentiation of Self

Bowen described this end of the scale:

".... *lower scale people are more vulnerable to stress and, for them, recovery from symptoms can be slow or impossible while higher scale people tend to recover rapidly.*[5]

"People in the lower half of the scale live in a "feeling" controlled world in which feelings and subjectivity are dominant over the objective reasoning process most of the time. They do not distinguish feeling from fact, and major life decisions are based on what "feels" right. Primary life goals are oriented around love, happiness, comfort and security; these goals come closest to fulfillment when relationships with others are in equilibrium. So much life energy goes into seeking love and approval, or attacking the other for not providing it, that there is little energy left for self-determined, goal-directed activity. They do not distinguish between "truth" and "fact," and the inner feeling state is the most accurate possible expression of truth. A sincere person is regarded as one who freely communicates the feeling process. An important life principle is "giving and receiving" love, attention and approval. Life can stay in symptom-free adjustment as long as the relationship system is in comfortable equilibrium. Chronic disruption of the relationship system results in dysfunction and a high incidence of human problems, including physical and emotional illness and social dysfunction."[6]

This description clearly sets out both kinds of fusion found at the lower end of the scale – relationship fusion and emotional/intellectual fusion. Not only do people at the lower end of the scale involve themselves in borrowing and lending of self, but their degree of anxiety results in fusion between the thinking and the feeling parts of the self. That is because their thinking is often "flooded" with emotion, making the thinking unreliable, biased, and based on subjectivity rather than on objective fact.

High Level Functioning

Further up the scale all this tends to reverse, progressively. Therefore, at higher levels, there is less relationship fusion, making relationships better-functioning. There are fewer life problems because people have fewer relationship difficulties and also because basing decisions more in fact than feeling makes for better long-term outcomes. So, in relationships, the more separate the selves, (the more out of the fusions) the better the relationships operate, and the better people feel more of the time. The more one is able to separate thinking and feeling, having some choice about which state one is in, the more reliable and accurate are perceptions of how things really are and the more decisions and planning will have desired outcomes.

The fusions themselves are the basis of measuring differentiation and undifferentiation. The more one fuses into relationships, the more undifferentiated one is. The more one separates from relationship fusions (over time, and with effort) the more differentiation is achieved. These relationship fusions are also, it is hypothesized, related to, if not responsible for, the thinking/feeling fusion. Now it becomes evident why the difficult words, "differentiation" and "undifferentiated" were chosen. They describe the situation perfectly!

A few of the indicators that have been used to assess life functioning are:

- Health (physical, emotional and social)

- Relationship success

- Life span

- "Success" (financial or contribution to society)

- Reproductive orderliness

- Educational attainment

- Ability to reach goals

None of these indicators can be taken alone to mean much, but they are based on facts that are more or less easily obtainable and together they give a picture of life lived at higher or lower levels on the scale. These are the facts people put on their family diagrams in order to get a picture of the functioning of their generations.

It is not possible to measure the level of differentiation, as Bowen said, because of the wide shifts in the functional level of pseudo-self in low-scale people. A compliment can raise the functioning and criticism can lower it.[7] Because of that phenomenon, differentiation can probably only be measured over a lifetime.

As people operate less and less out of emotional fusions with significant others, freed of the relationship anxiety generated by the fused condition, they report that their relationships function better than ever before. It's not that they are free of emotion, or automatic behavior (who is?) but that they have more choice over what and when they feel, think and do. All this tends to improve relationships greatly.

Since fusion is the idea on which the idea of differentiation is based, let's look at it a little closer.

Relationship Fusions

Relationship fusions result from the mutual giving up and/or taking on – exchange of – selves that occurs when people become important to each other. Relationships are more fused at the lower end of the scale and less so progressing upwards. Also, anxiety passes more easily between the individuals in fusions with each other than it does with other people. Remember the cows? The anxiety stayed relatively within the fence, within that particular herd. That is because the individuals in that herd, by virtue of spending time together, were important to each other – they were part of an emotional unit.

Besides passing anxiety easily between themselves, people in fusions are there for each other, at a feeling level, in a reactive way that they are not for other people. They participate in the relationship patterns when the anxiety is up. We may find ourselves reactively agreeing with someone – or disagreeing with them – simply because of the relationship fusion we are in rather than based on the facts or the logical content of the topic.

This phenomenon leaves one vulnerable to groupthink – going along with the group based only on relationship reasons rather than on any principle, logic or original thought one may have on the subject. Or, reactive to groupthink, one could reactively disagree even though not having thought through the issue.

How does one's fusion-ability develop? Theoretically, we each come out of our original families with whatever degree of fusion capacity (undifferentiation) we will carry throughout life. (Figures 8 and 9)

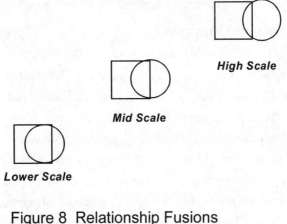

High Scale

Mid Scale

Lower Scale

Figure 8 Relationship Fusions

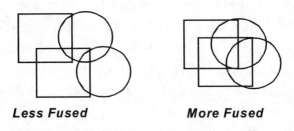

Less Fused   **More Fused**

Figure 9 Different Degrees of Family Fusion

Family Togetherness

In the families in which we grow up, there are more or less demands for togetherness. Lower scale families are caught in more togetherness, have higher anxiety levels more of the time and are less comfortable with their members as autonomous individuals. They demand so much, relationally, of their members, that they have little left over with which to cope with the rest of life's challenges or to make a contribution of their own. About all people at lowest levels of human functioning can do is to try to get through each day. Parent-child relationships in these families may tend towards over-focus, or if the family is on "overwhelm," neglect. In either situation, the offspring can develop symptoms of various kinds, lack boundaries, get ill, and/or show an inability to stay within the rules of society.

Higher scale families, on the other hand, promote autonomy, are less anxious with their children as individuals – their questions, explorations, creative ventures and variation in general. They carry less anxiety. The children are given enough protection for their realistic needs, but neither too much, nor too little focus. Eventually they emerge less fused into the family emotionally, freer to be a self. (Partly that means they are freer to know what they think, independent of their systems.) This means they reach adulthood with more self available to themselves (instead of tied up in the group's emotional demands). They have more life energy to deal with life's challenges, reach goals, and create their own nuclear unit, relatively free of anxiety.

The two ends of the scale do not define the many levels on the scale between the extremes, but it is understood that all those nuances exist – the scale is truly a spectrum.

With that understanding of how variation in differentiation of self looks and comes about, we are in a position to look at an illustration of the theoretical construct of the self.

Components of the Self

Another useful way of seeing the differences in individuals is in the form of a diagram developed by Kathleen Kerr, based on Bowen theory. The diagram makes it easier to visualize the differentiation/undifferentiation tension that exists within all of us. (Figure 10)[8]

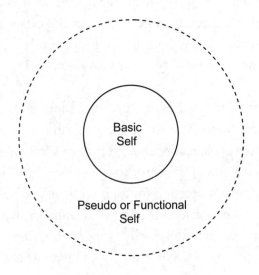

Figure 10 Basic and Pseudo Self

The diagram consists of four major components, all intricately linked:

- Pseudo- or functional self,

- Basic or solid self,

- Boundaries around each, and

- Guiding principles for each (not usually diagrammed but important).

Pseudo-self

Bowen described the pseudo-self this way: *"The pseudo-self, acquired under the influence of the relationship system, is negotiable in the relationship system."[9]*

Pseudo- or functional self is where most of us live, most of the time. It is the part that participates in the relationship exchange involved in fusions. It is the immature, automatic, thoughtless reactivity in us. It lets in the anxiety from the system, functions on borrowed self from another, or conversely, gives up self to another in an instant. It is the togetherness force within us.

Within it, guiding it to some extent, are the unexamined precepts adopted from one's culture, family or friends. Some examples of these might include racist stereotypes, blind acceptance of a political position, or not-thought-through religious beliefs. As Bowen said, *[It is] " . . . made up of a mass of heterogeneous facts, beliefs and principles acquired through the relationship system in the prevailing emotion. These include facts learned because one is supposed to know them, and beliefs borrowed from others or accepted in order to enhance one's position in relationship to others."[10]*

However, many of these are outside of awareness and can hardly be counted as principles. Then too, for pseudo-self, the most important guiding "influence" is simply the relationship system itself, with all of its pressure to be included, liked, or a "team player." As goes the system, so goes that self. It can adopt an unthinking cooperative, "groupthink" attitude. But, conversely, it can react to the lending of self inherent in that position, and adopt a stance that goes against the group automatically.

Lower on the scale, more of the self will consist of pseudo-self, or undifferentiation. Higher on the scale, the pseudo-self will be smaller.

Basic Self

The differentiated part of self – basic self (sometimes called solid self) – is the part that vies with pseudo-self against togetherness and for individuality. It is the best that is in us. It constantly prods us to go on to do better.

Let's hear Bowen: *"The basic self is a definite quality illustrated by such 'I position stances as: 'These are my beliefs and convictions. This is what I am and who I am and what I will do, or not do.'"* [11]

The basic self does not take part in the borrowing or loss of self in relationships.

It stays objective, basing decisions and judgments on fact.

Basic self, always present in converse proportions to pseudo-self, is larger at higher levels on the scale and smaller at lower levels.

Basic self is guided by well thought-through *principles*, arrived at through the best thinking, based on logic and fact, that one can do. It is not subject to group or relationship pressure. Martin Luther's famous statement, "Here I stand!" would be an example of how the guiding principles operate to direct basic self.

Guiding principles of the basic self are examined in the crucible of living, over time, to see how reliable they actually are.

Though not vulnerable to emotional pressure, these guiding principles are not rigid. They are capable of changing as new data become available.

The principle-led life (as well as principle-led parents, leaders and therapists) will be very different from that led by relationship pressures. Today, it is, sadly, rare to see public, or any leaders, who are principle-led.

Boundaries

The boundaries of pseudo-self may be described as permeable. Self and anxiety leak through them easily. The higher on the scale the person, the less permeable are the boundaries of pseudo-self. The lower on the scale, the more permeable they are. (Figure 11)

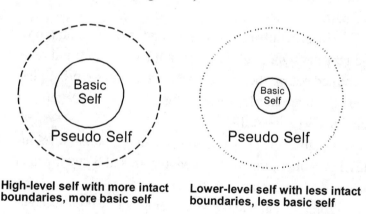

High-level self with more intact boundaries, more basic self   **Lower-level self with less intact boundaries, less basic self**

Figure 11 Low and High Level Selfs

On the other hand, the boundaries of the basic self are not permeable, since the basic or solid part of the self does not take part in exchanges of self or anxiety in relationships. Basic self takes on the other's emotion by choice. It is not an automatic response.

Guiding principles

Because they are so important, let us summarize and contrast the different types of guidance available. Both pseudo- and basic-self have guidance, but only the basic self is guided by actual thought-through principles that are in the awareness of the person. Those of the pseudo-self are absorbed from the culture, parents and other important systems. Since they are unexamined and often out of awareness, the person does not realize what is guiding him/her. Usually it is simply the perceived and/or real relationship pressures of whatever system of which he/she is a part.

The principles of basic self, on the other hand are well thought-through, put to the test in life over time, and re-examined before they become adopted as basic principles. The principle-led life is very different from the system- or relationship-guided life.

Again, there is a spectrum, depending upon level of differentiation, of how much people are led by their principles and how much by the system.

Some examples of people being led by their principles will be described in the last chapter.

Differentiating a Self

A knowledge of Bowen family systems theory is extremely useful in the effort to move up the scale of differentiation of self. The better one is able to understand theory, the more one can use it and the more it becomes a way of thinking about life. There is no substitute for becoming well-grounded in theory.

Out of the rich concepts of Bowen theory come a whole host of ways to work on gaining more basic self, and living less out of pseudo-self.

Primary among these is, of course, going back to one's family and working on self there. The most effective place to change relationship or personality difficulties is in the system where they first developed. Coaching by someone familiar with theory is essential to this effort.

Since anxiety figures so large in relationship dilemmas, many people add to this the effort to work on the regulation of anxiety by such methods as relaxation training, biofeedback or various stress management techniques.

All that has been learned about working on self in one's own family can be applied in any system – one's nuclear family, a workplace, a university, a hospital or a congregation.

Leadership

From these ideas it is clear that there can be such things as high and low level leaders (or parents). High level leaders:

- lead by their principles (but don't beat people over the head with them),

- stay grounded in facts and thinking out

- stay in good contact with appropriate people in the system.

Freer of relationship anxiety, this leader or parent can make good decisions.

Thinking systems, and seeing emotional process, one can see one's place in the system more objectively. Usually, unless one gets out of contact, the system will be grateful for someone working on self in this way.

Coaching

Differentiation of self is the goal of Bowen theory-based coaching. This is very different from most other therapies, the mission of which is usually symptom removal. As people work on differentiation, however, it is interesting and encouraging to see symptoms drop away. As people work on getting to a better level, they carry less anxiety, which is at the base of most symptoms. They make better decisions, often at issue in human difficulties. They are more effective in relationships and relationship systems.

In coaching, or psychotherapy, if one is working on differentiation of self, one relates differently to persons in consultation. Relating from principle rather than emotional patterns, bringing people back to the basics of Bowen theory whenever possible, is very useful. In the scale of differentiation of self, they will be challenged in a way they have not been in other types of therapy. They will see new ways of approaching cultural, relationship and other life dilemmas. They will be grateful for coaching through this lens.

For coaches, their own coaching experience will be essential, though didactic learning as well as reading as much as possible in and about theory are also needed if one is to begin coaching according to principles of Bowen theory.

Most of us, even though well grounded in theory, find it useful to create opportunities for exposure to other system thinkers on a long term basis.

NOTES

[1] Bowen, "Family Therapy in Clinical Practice" Aronson, 1978, 1983, 1985 New York, p. 472.

[2] Kathleen Kerr has been given access to the Goodall research data and sees evidence in the chimpanzees, for different levels of functioning in different individuals. She has reported on this work at many meetings at the Bowen Center for the Study of the Family, Washington, D.C.

[3] Bowen, op. cit.

[4] Bowen, op cit, p.473.

[5] Bowen, op cit, p. 472.

[6] Bowen, op cit p.473-474.

[7] Ibid, p. 366.

[8] Kerr, Kathleen, in lectures given at the Bowen Center for the Study of the Family (then the Georgetown Family Center) in 1987-88.

[9] Bowen op cit p.473.

[10] Ibid.

[11] Ibid.

3

TRIANGLES

"The theory states that the triangle, a three-person emotional configuration, is the molecule or the basic building block of any emotional system, whether it is in the family or any other group. The triangle is the smallest stable relationship system. A two-person system may be stable as long as it is calm, but when anxiety increases, it immediately involves the most vulnerable other person to become a triangle. When tension in the triangle is too great for the threesome, it involves others to become a series of interlocking triangles."[1]

Murray Bowen, 1976

Triangles – another extremely important concept. In fact, triangles are so important that they appear in Bowen theory five times! (They are ubiquitous not only in life but also in theory.) Not only do triangles come up over and over again when we think about families – or organizations – but they, being the smallest stable unit of an emotional system, are the building blocks upon which all of society itself is built.

Because they are more complex, triangles are more difficult to understand than two-person relationships. There are more data points to keep in mind. Moreover, they are constantly "lighting up" in different ways so that just as one thinks one understands what is going on, the triangle changes.

All this goes back to day one in our own families. For all of us, the experience of the triangles has been repetitive and cumulative. This personal experience can contribute to our understanding of them if we allow ourselves to step back, take a good look and then think about what we have seen.

In a group of any size, the number of possible triangles that can be drawn among all the different players is astounding. It is a good exercise to try. However, one will never begin to understand systems like a family, and certainly, even larger organizations, unless one can gain some facility with the idea of triangles. So let's take them on.

Like the other concepts, they derive from the first one, "Nuclear Family Emotional System." There, triangles are first set out in the form of the "child focus." The child focus is no doubt the simplest, clearest example of a triangle in an emotional system. Let's review.

The Child Focus Triangle

A parent is upset. The second parent "takes on" the upset. A child, by being near that parent, takes on the anxiety. It may happen several times a day in any family. But if it becomes a pattern, the family ends up with an anxious child. If the anxiety lasts long enough, the child will develop a symptom. That symptom will only draw more anxiety from the parents, adding to the burden of anxiety on the child, and so on and on. The problem and the anxiety intensify as time goes by. This original triangle is useful to remember from time to time as a paradigm of the idea of triangles. (Figure 12)

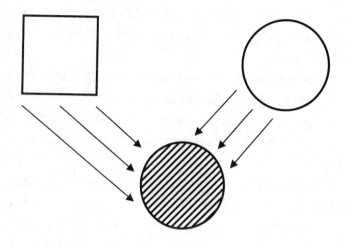

Figure 12 Triangling

Triangles in Other Species

Triangles are not difficult to find in the natural world. One of the most dramatic examples is found in Frans deWaal's "Chimpanzee Politics," when Luit and Nikki joined forces to unseat the reigning monarch, Yeroen.[2] Again, in de Waal's "Peacemaking Among Primates" Mama was known for her peacemaking abilities. She would take two warring parties, one in each arm, to stop the fighting. Eventually they would do the chimp version of "kiss and make up."[3]

Triangles in the Family

For all of us, understanding triangles in the human family is based on living in them. Triangles are ubiquitous. They are not good. They are not bad. Like other patterns of human relatedness, they just are. They are automatic, a part of the picture.

It is not a matter of whether we are in triangles. We always are in them, if the anxiety is up even a little. When the system is calm, they are still there, in the shadows, waiting to come out of hiding when anxiety increases again.

As Bowen said, *"A three-person system is one triangle, a four person system is four primary triangles, a five-person system is nine primary triangles, etc. This progression multiplies rapidly as systems get larger. In addition, there are a variety of secondary triangles when two or more may band together for one corner of a triangle for one emotional issue, while the configuration shifts on another issue."[4]*

When two people become anxious, they triangle in a third. Have you ever noticed the automaticity of the phenomenon at a conference? In the midst of an animated discussion with someone in the hallway, the author often wonders, "How long before someone else joins in?" It usually happens immediately following the thought! Two intense people cannot resist the urge to bring someone else in. No one, on the other hand, can resist the urge to join two intense others. It's automatic. It's human.

Bowen: *". . .In periods of calm, the triangle is made up of a comfortably close twosome and a less comfortable outsider. The twosome work to preserve the togetherness, lest one become uncomfortable and form a better together-ness elsewhere. The outsider seeks to form a togetherness with one of the twosome, and there are numerous well-known moves to accomplish this. The emotional forces within the triangle are constantly in motion from moment to moment, even in periods of calm. . .Moderate tension states in the twosome are characteristically felt by one, while the other is oblivious. It is the uncomfortable one who initiates a new equilibrium toward more comfortable togetherness for self. In periods of stress, the outside position is the most comfortable and desired position."*[5]

What are the "numerous well-known moves" through which outsiders in triangles seek to form togetherness with another? Gossip is a favorite, right along with rumor-mongering or making insinuations.

It is useful for anyone to remind oneself, when the anxiety is up, to resist the urge to be in the middle of it, not feeling "left out" when outside the intensity. It is actually the preferable position. One can learn more a little outside the triangles, looking in. It can be viewed as a test of one's level of functioning.

Triangles can build on themselves, interlock, and then polarize so that a whole extended family or large organization can become involved in taking sides over a supposed issue. Interestingly, experience shows that the "issue" is rarely triggering the anxiety. When the real source of the anxiety trigger can be discovered and met appropriately, often the crisis in the family or organization is over. (Figure 13)

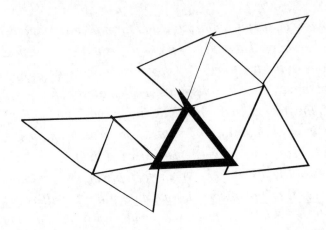

Figure 13 Triangles Can Interlock and Polarize
Detriangling

From the ubiquitous nature of triangles it becomes
apparent that there is no such thing as "detriangling,"
except in the most relative sense. In that relative sense, it is
important, however, in the midst of intense triangling, to
work to get to a calmer, more "outside" position. In this
position, one becomes more the observer. In the observing
mode, one becomes emotionally calmer, a little more able
to think objectively. This is hard work, but most useful for
the individual trying to get to a better level of differentiation as well as for the whole group. Of course, one
individual working on self in this way benefits the entire
group.

In any emotionally intense situation it is useful to ask
"Where's the triangle?" Upon reflection, one will usually
become obvious. The ensuing work may not be easy but it

will seem less complicated for knowing the nature of the beast.

Once one knows the triangle involved, is observing and relatively calm and objective, what then? Is there any action to take? A few pointers include:

- From calm thoughtfulness and emotional neutrality, stay in contact with each of the other two angles of the triangle.

- Put them together in your thinking and talk – "I know the two of you can solve this."

- Remembering that in intense situations, the outside position is the preferable one. Asking questions about additional facts can be a good way of keeping that calm, "outside" position.

Coaching

The triangle can be used in a positive way for the system. (Calm is "catching," too.)

Bowen stressed the value of observation: *"The therapeutic system is based on being able to observe accurately to see the part that self plays, and to consciously control this programmed emotional reactiveness. The observation and the control are equally difficult. Observation is not possible until one can control one's reactions sufficiently to be able to observe. The process of observation allows for more control, which in turn, in a series of slow steps, allows for better observation. . . It is only when one can get a little outside that it is possible to begin to observe . . .When there is finally one who can*

*control his emotional responsiveness and not take sides
with either of the other two, and stay constantly in contact
with the other two, their emotional intensity within the
twosome will decrease and both will move to a higher level
of differentiation. Unless the triangled person can remain
in emotional contact, the twosome will triangle in someone
else."[6]*

Bowen theory-guided coaches intentionally create
and then get out of a triangle in marriage consultations.
They relate to each partner in turn from a neutral position.
As they do this with the other partner watching, the
intensities of the fusions are calmed. People can begin to
think and solve problems.

Some will actually take up the work of defining and
differentiating a self.

Parents and Leaders

Just as parents are the best coaches for the family, *the
leader of the organization or congregation is the best
coach for it.* For that reason, consultants to organizations
do best to work primarily with the leaders. And, leadership
is partly, at least, about learning to better define self to the
organization. Partly, that involves *staying emotionally neutral in triangles, while finding a way to communicate,
based on one's principles, what one thinks to each.* When
the calm third (coach, parent or leader of the organization)
can remain in contact with the other two, they gradually
begin to de-escalate. At that point they can think. Logical
thinking, after all, is how they will solve their problems
with each other and in the system generally.

The classic descriptions (of the coach remaining calm and in good contact with both the others) are a great way for anyone to think about managing oneself in intense triangles. They are with us everywhere, so we all will have plenty of opportunities to practice. *As we manage self toward becoming and being that calming, thinking, self-defining presence, connected with the others, we not only go up on the scale, we find that they come up to join us, over time.*

Certainly, a calm, thinking, principled leader can have a positive effect upon intense triangles. It is hard work, but extremely rewarding. One cannot help but wonder – how many leaders, knowing and using this concept, would it take to have an impact on the dire social problems we face today?

NOTES

[1] Bowen, M "Family Therapy in Clinical Practice," Aronson New York, p. 373.
[2] deWaal, Frans, "Chimpanzee Politics" Johns Hopkins Press, Baltimore and London, Ch's. 2 and 3.
[3] deWaal, Frans, "Peacemaking Among Primates" Harvard University Press Cambridge and London p. 42.
[4] Bowen, op cit p. 479.
[5] Ibid.
[6] Ibid, p. 480.

4

CUTOFF

"An average family situation in our society today is one in which people maintain a distant and formal relationship with the family of origin, returning home for duty visits at infrequent intervals." [1]

Murray Bowen, 1976

Cutoff was noticed by Bowen in the 1960's when large numbers of teenagers were running away from home, hitchhiking across the country. Cutoff is a *"process of separation, isolation, withdrawal, running away, or denying the importance of the parental family."* [2] Strictly speaking, it originally referred to an intergenerational phenomenon. In practice, however, it is used to refer to any significant relationship that shows the pattern. (Figure 14)

Figure 14 Cutoff

Cutoff is the extreme form of the distance posture described in the first concept. When a relationship becomes sufficiently emotionally intense, at some point, people will often cut off internally or geographically. Communications cease. It often leads to symptoms but it is seldom recognized for its part in the problem. It can be crept into, after years of more and more distancing, or it can be a sudden reaction to a conflict that has reached proportions that someone defines as untenable for the continuation of the relationship. It can be mutual, where both parties want it and participate, or it can be unilateral – desired by one person and not the other.

In most families there are branches to whom we are related but have no idea because of a cutoff that occurred generations before. As the people reproduced they created branches of the same family who do not communicate nor even know each other exists! Cutoff is so prevalent among us that America has been called "a nation of cutoffs." That has to do with the large number of immigrants living in this country and the high incidence of cutoff present in immigration in general. (Of course, there is by no means a 100% correlation between immigration and cutoff, since geographical separation does not imply lack of contact, especially with today's availability of means of communication.)

What Leads to Cutoff?

The degree to which one is fused with (undifferentiated from) one's parents leaves one with a tendency toward all the relationship patterns, since they are symptoms of the fusions. Cutoff is one of the ways people attempt to resolve the relationship tension that results from that unresolved attachment (fusion or undifferentiation) and the anxiety it engenders. Fusions do not feel comfortable, so people have a tendency to want to get away from them, to cut off. As Bowen said: *"The degree of unresolved attachment to the parents is equivalent to the degree of undifferentiation that must somehow be handled in the person's own life and in future generations."*[3] (Figure 15)

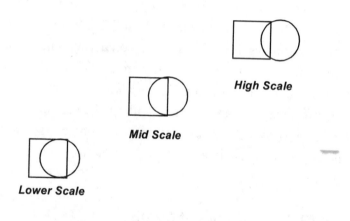

High Scale

Mid Scale

Lower Scale

Figure 15 Relationship Fusions

Descriptions of Cutoff

"The unresolved attachment is handled by the intra-psychic process of denial and isolation of self while living close to the parents: or by physically running away: or by a combination of emotional isolation and physical distance. The more intense the cutoff with the past the more likely the individual to have an exaggerated version of his parental

*family problem in his own marriage, and the more likely
his own children to do a more intense cutoff with him in the
next generation. There are many variations in the intensity
of the basic process and in the way the cutoff is handled.*[4]

The person who cuts off from his or her family is not
any more independent that the one who never leaves home.
They are both reactive to a huge degree of fusion. Relationship "nomads," or serial monogamists and hermits all
represent versions of intense cutoff. One who cuts off from
parents is vulnerable to impulsively getting into an emotionally intense marriage that ends in the cutoff of divorce.[5]

So, only as any of us stays in contact with his or her
family or origin and its past generations, will we do as well
as possible in life. The same is true of our children. If one
cuts off, it can become a family pattern. The children will
be likely to cut off and then all will show the effects of that
cutoff – an increase in anxiety and various symptoms as a
result.

The Biphasic Nature of Cutoff

While it feels so good initially to be rid of that
troublesome family, over time, cutoff, like all the other
relationship patterns, creates anxiety. Anxiety, as we have
seen, leads to symptoms. In the long term anxiety sets in, in
the form of depression or other symptoms. It will not be
seen as related to the cutoff from family. In the first place,
the cutoff felt so good. Secondly, the symptom's onset is
often far removed in time from the beginning of the cutoff,
so the logical connection is not made.

Dr. Baker's Research

Dr. Katharine Baker studied the effects of cutoff at the University of Moscow.[6] There, many people of one generation had been killed in Stalin's "purges." When records in Russia were opened, many people showed a great deal of interest in finding out all they could about this, their (by now) grandparent generation.

As predicted, those who knew most, or showed the most interest in finding out about their grandparent generation were also functioning the best. Those who knew less and showed less interest (an evidence of cutoff) were doing less well in their life functioning. Dr. Baker's research tends to vindicate the original theoretical descriptions of cutoff and its effects on functioning.

The Group Home Experience

Another study, done by the author, was small but again highlighted the importance of the concept of cutoff.[7] In a group home treatment facility where 10 to 15 adolescent girls lived, the director and staff realized that, after being separated from their homes for treatment, cutoff was being promoted. This was thought to be a result of staff attitudes that are common in such agencies and in society in general (tacit parent-blaming when children have problems). In addition, contact between the residents and their families was not being encouraged to the degree it might be. We were not thinking systems.

As the staff learned something about Bowen family systems theory counselors encouraged more frequent contact between the girls and their families. This was accomplished by phone calls, letters and by at least monthly in-person visits. (The agency drew from a large region.)

As a result of this initiative we noticed significant changes. Grades in school went up overall. Medication doses went down. There were dramatically fewer emergencies, such as absconding, cutting, suicide attempts and conflicts requiring the director to come in from home. The director, who carried a pager as a part of her job description, so that she could respond in person to such events, exclaimed, "I almost never get paged any more! The house is a very different place."

Grief or Cutoff?

The author has watched as people have put the principles into practice around the death of an important person. The conclusion seems inescapable, though formal research has not been done as yet, that it is family emotional cutoff, rather than the grief per se, that accounts for the classical stages of the "grieving process" often described, first by Freud and then Kubler-Ross and others.

When survivors stay connected with the extended family of the deceased (the emotional unit of which he or she was a part), they have a very different grief experience. I believe it is the cutoff from that unit (of which the deceased individual was only a small fragment, after all) that produces the more intense and protracted grief reactions. By maintaining contact with the dead spouse's family of origin, survivors stay in contact with the emotional process that is still very much alive and well in that unit, the unit of which he or she had been a part.

Coaching

The implications of the concept of cutoff for coaching others are obvious. However, it is only as the coach works on bridging his or her own family cutoffs that he or she will have the sensitivity it takes to act as a guide for others in bridging their cutoffs. This is one example of the many positive effects of working on self in one's own family. There really is no substitute for that hard work. It is a prerequisite for the coach (who will need a coach to ford these sometimes white waters) but the enormous payoffs, not only in coaching, but in all of life, make it more than worthwhile.

Leadership

Leaders need to be addressing their own family cutoffs as well as those in their organizations. Inevitably, in any organization of any size, there will be some individuals at the periphery who may not be in communication with the larger group. One might hypothesize that, the larger the group, corporations, universities, or congregations might be more at risk for fostering cutoff. Knowing about the concept will guide the leadership. They need to make certain that the leadership relationships themselves are in good contact. After that, they can ensure that they make contact with the rest of the large group through regular contact with the leaders of various smaller groups within the organization. The organization will also need to make an effort to make contact with the community of which it is a part if it is to be the highest functioning organization possible.

NOTES

[1] Bowen, M, "Family Therapy in Clinical Practice" (New York: Aronson), p. 383.

[2] Ibid p. 383.

[3] Ibid, p. 382.

[4] Ibid, p. 382.

[5] Ibid, p. 382, 383.

[6] Baker, K., "The Effects of Stalin's Purges on Three Generations of Russian Families," *Family Systems* (Georgetown Family Center, Spring/Fall, 1996, Vol. 3, no.1), pp. 5-35.

[7] Gilbert, R., "Addressing Cutoff in Residential Care of Disturbed Adolescents" *Family Systems,* Fall, 2002.

5

FAMILY PROJECTION PROCESS

"The process through which parental undifferentia-tion impairs one or more children operates within the father-mother-child triangle . . . It exists in all gradations of intensity, from those in which impairment is minimal to those in which the child is seriously impaired for life. The process is so universal it is present to some degree in all families."[1]

Murray Bowen, 1976

Now let's take a closer look at that original triangle we saw as the child focus in chapter 1. This time, we'll look not only at how it affects one child, but we will see how that child focus affects all the children in the family.

Most of us have at some time wondered at the infinite variety that is possible in the family. "How can functioning levels of children of the same two parents be so different?" We all know examples of siblings who show extreme con-trast from each other, to the point of one having schizo-phrenic-level functioning and the other being a high-level leader. Many, if not most, families display a wide range of functioning in their offspring. When one adds the fact, from family systems theory, that two people marry at exactly the same level of differentiation, the sibling spectrum scatter becomes all the more incomprehensible and intriguing.

The concept of the family projection process concerns itself with just that phenomenon. It explains how differentiation levels are passed from parents to offspring as well as how that process can be different for each child in the family.

How Can Siblings Be So Different?

Why do offspring of the same family turn out so different? Often people conclude that "They all have the same parents so it can't have anything to do with the parents!" They put the responsibility for shaping children's lives for successful or risky behavior on outside forces, such as the culture, the media, or – peer pressure.[2]

However, the largest research study ever done, the "Add Health" Study,[3] found peers to be an influence, but they were far down the list when different factors were ranked in importance. The researchers found the relationship with parents to be by far the most important factor in whether teenagers engage in risky behavior such as drugs or sex.

Is it sibling position that makes for individual differences in functioning? Certainly sibling position in the family accounts for some percentage of personality differences. It shows how weaknesses, strengths and even relationship tendencies can be shaped in our original family by the order we were born into it. It demonstrates also, how differently each sibling experiences his or her family experience. For example, the oldest can often remember a time when he or she was an only child. The youngest is aware of no time when there was not someone older, or "over" him or her.

(Sibling position and its effect on personality is explored in greater detail in chapter 7.)

But though it holds statistically, in the individual case, the concept of sibling position is not that instructive when it comes to life functioning. People in any position in the family can have a successful life course, or they may not do so well. Each position has strengths and weaknesses. But what makes the difference in how those strengths are used and the weaknesses managed so that one does better or not?

Differentiation of Self and The Child Focus

Of course, through the lens of Bowen theory, by definition, one's level of differentiation of self makes for success in life, or the lack thereof. That level can be quite different among siblings. It is true in almost any family one can think of. But, exactly how does it happen that children of the same parents vary so widely in their ability to cope with life, realize potential and reach goals – their levels of differentiation?

Bowen theory answers the question by means of the "child focus" – the triangle that makes all the difference. Remember how anxiety, and thus, sometimes, symptoms end up in a child? (Figure 16)

That worried focus, or "projection" of anxiety is how anxiety gets off-loaded to offspring. If one worries excessively about one's child (or reacts to an overload of anxiety by neglect, or over-focuses in an over-positive manner) one transmits – or projects – that anxiety directly onto the child.

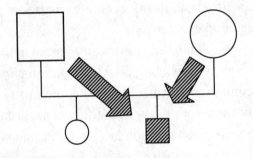

Figure 16 Child Focus Process

Variation in the Same Family

It seems that *the projection process is different for different children.* We as parents worry about (or neglect or unrealistically "adore") some of our children more than others. Parents say that some children "draw" more focus than others. The focus may be over-negative, (angry or worried) neglectful, or over-positive. The valence (positive or negative) doesn't seem to matter. (Figure 17)

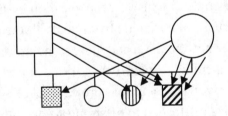

Figure 17 Variations in Child Focus

In that way, different children can end up with differing amounts of inappropriate focus. The more a child is on the receiving end of a worried, over-positive focus (or around a parent so anxious as to be neglectful) the greater the anxiety transmitted, and thus the fusion of selves with the parent(s). *The greater the fusion, the lower the level of differentiation of self.*

In any family, a given child can receive so much focus (anxiety) that other siblings are left a little freer of the family emotional process. They will receive less anxiety. Thus, they are less fused into the family self-amalgam (are less a part of the family emotional process). At the same time, they do not cut off from it. They are in communication with it. They recognize the problems, and they, too, carry some of the spillover anxiety, just not as much. With less anxiety to deal with, they develop more basic self to go out and do whatever their talents call for in the world.

In Other Species

In Dr. Jane Goodalls's observations of the Gombe Stream chimpanzees, she reports the fascinating story of Flo and Flint. Flo, the mother, a high ranking female, had reared several other successful and high ranking offspring. By the time Flint came along, she was old and tired. He was indulged by her to an unusual degree. Flint refused to separate from her, riding on her back long past the time that is usually seen in chimps. When she died, Flint refused to leave the spot where his mother died, dying there himself three weeks later.[4]

Factors Influencing the Projection Process

How do we understand the initiation of the projections? What magnetizes parents' anxiety more toward one child than another?

It may be that at the time of birth, because of special circumstances, anxiety is very high. As we know, anxiety is not always dealt with in logical ways. Sometimes it is diverted around the system. This is not a thought-through process, enacted by a family in order to "do in" one of its children. Rather, it is entirely out of awareness. It is automatic. If the anxiety is high at the time of the birth of a child, however, it can circuit around the emotional unit, triggering an over-focus on the child. Once it gets started, the over-focus tends to perpetuate itself.

Sometimes, the youngest, or the oldest, gets the focus simply because he or she is there to receive it, the others being out of the home, or not having arrived yet.

Or, a parent may have grown up with a sibling with a problem and then fear illogically, but intensely, that his or her own child in that same position (the oldest, the third, the middle, etc.) might develop the problem. That fear can turn into an over focus.

Still other families are faced with a child with a *difference,* a special problem or handicap that may draw the parental anxiety. Sometimes the adopted one is "chosen."

The good news is that: *"A child who grows up relatively outside the family projection process can emerge with a higher basic level of differentiation than the parents"*[5]

This being the case, it is one more great reason for us all to learn to process our anxiety as individuals, rather than passing it around the family system.

A Blameless Process

Some might hear the family projection process as blaming the parents for the child's problems. If they are projecting anxiety, aren't they at fault?

Not at all. The family projection process is not intentional, it is entirely automatic. Parents have no idea of their part in the problem. Often, however, when they learn about the concept and that they are contributing unwittingly to the problem, they are able to modify their part to some extent with wonderful results.

Not only is the process automatic and out of awareness, it has to do with their connectedness into their generations. They, too, were the recipients of parental anxiety, and their parents before them. The process is too big in all of our families to leave room for blame.

Observations of emotional processes in a given family are not made for the purpose of condemnation. They do, however, often make it possible for the present generation, when people can see how they play a part, however unintentional, to have more choices, and thus leave a different legacy for their offspring.

Coaching

The concept of the family projection process has shown itself to be extremely useful to some parents. Depending, of course on level of differentiation, some families can hear this concept and do something about an over focus on one or more of their children. Often, as parents become more involved in their own pursuits (especially that of a higher level of differentiation) resolving, instead of projecting anxiety and working on their own relationships – in their own marriages and families of origin – the child will behave like a bird let out of a cage, dropping symptoms and showing better development. Interestingly, before that happens some children will show an intensifying of the symptom, as if they are trying to "draw" the focus back. That reaction will be short-lived if the parents are warned ahead of time that it may happen, and stay on course with their own efforts to pull up in functioning.

Parents understanding how they perceive and react emotionally to different children differently can, with effort, get the focus off the kids and back on to themselves and their own adult relationships.

The coach's own thoughtful understanding and emotionally calm connectedness promotes ability to think through and thus lessen patterned behavior.

Leaders

Because they are in a unique position in the system, leaders are different from the group. Sometimes that is all it takes in an emotional system to initiate a focus. Leaders are singled out for it on a regular basis. They can and will, if they are thinking systems, expect and prepare for it rather than be taken by surprise, as victims. Members of the group may try to press the leader into unrealistic roles, and when he or she does not meet the expectations, they react. This kind of situation presents a wonderful opportunity to meet reactivity with calm connectedness.

Members of the group who have been the object of an over-focus in the triangles of their families of origin can repeat the emotional process of that family in other groups by drawing focus.

Leaders, too, can take part in an over focus on an employee or staff person, leading to a loss of function in that person. People tend to live up (or down) to expectations.

One has choices about what to do with anxiety – both that which originates within oneself and that which is passed to one from the group. One can deal with it, resolving it within self – the responsible action to take. Or, one can pass it along through the triangles of the system, inciting further anxiety in the system, making more of a problem for oneself in the long run.

Again, theory shows the way out. If we know theory, we can use it, if we don't, we can't.

One way out of the family projection process is to work for a bigger picture of the family emotional process – that is, to look at the preceding generations to see what can be learned. Of course, if cutoffs get bridged in the bargain, that is all to the good.

Now, let's take a look at how the projection process goes through the generations.

NOTES

[1] Bowen, M, *Family Therapy in Clinical Practice* (New York: Aronson, 1989), p.379.

[2] Harris, J "The Nurture Assumption" Free Press 1998. The author makes the case that parents have little or nothing to do with how offspring turn out. Peer pressure, in her opinion, is much more significant.

[3] This study was sponsored by the National Institutes of Health and involved 90,000 young people and 20,000 families. It published its first results in 1997 and is still in progress. See Add Health - NIH Website.

[4] Goodall, J *The Chimpanzees of Gombe* Harvard Cambridge MA 1986 pp. 103, 204. Mrs Kathleen Kerr has been granted access to the Goodall research data and at present is analyzing and interpreting those studies through the lens of Bowen theory. See www.thejanedoodall.org.

[5] Bowen, op cit p.477.

MULTIGENERATIONAL TRANSMISSION PROCESS

"The family projection process continues through multiple generations. In any nuclear family, there is one child who is the primary object of the family projection process. This child emerges with a lower level of differentiation than the parents and does less well in life. Other children, who are minimally involved with the parents, emerge with about the same levels of differentiation as the parents. Those who grow up relatively outside the family emotional process develop better levels of differentiation than the parents. If we follow the most impaired child through successive generations, we will see one line of descent producing lower and lower levels of differentiation . . . If we followed the line through the children who emerge with about the same levels of differentiation, we see a remarkable consistency of family functioning through the generations. . . If we follow the multigenerational lineage of those who emerge with higher levels of differentiation, we will see a line of highly functioning and very successful people."

Murray Bowen, 1976[1]

Once more, it is especially easy to see how the concepts of Bowen theory proceed, one out of the other. If the family projection process explains how differentiation – and undifferentiation – is passed from one generation to another, the multigenerational transmission process is simply that same phenomenon, writ large, through the generations.

In Other Species?

Does anxiety pass through the generations in other species? Not enough research into this question has been done to know for sure, partly because the higher mammals live too long for a researcher to follow many generations. But since we saw something like the family projection process (upon which this concept is an expansion) occurring in the Goodall chimps, there is no reason to think that variation would not be passed along many generations.

Emotional Process in Families

Different levels of differentiation in different siblings can give rise to whole branches of families that are ascending, or descending on the scale.

Again, it is the enormity of this phenomenon that makes us realize that we are all only a small part of something much larger than ourselves. Many people are too cut off to take much interest in their generations. But for those who do, there is great reward. They constantly demonstrate it in their lives.

Observing the Generations

Many start their research with the oldest members of their families. This is a rich, connecting experience for most. Most of the older relatives are glad someone wants to know, and that their knowledge will not die with them. In just connecting with these members, people report gleaning the benefits of bridging cutoffs – feeling more connected, more grounded, functioning better.

After that, many will become interested in genealogy. Genealogy is important and there are many helps for this search now available. But putting the emotional process as flesh on the genealogy bones will, in the end, go far towards making present day emotional process of the family make sense. How do we do that?

The Family Diagram

In looking at the generations of our families, we are looking for facts. Emotion-colored stories are interesting, but have to be evaluated for factual reliability. It is those facts that will tell a story about differentiation. Important facts include, names, of course, as well as:

- Longevity of family members

- Health

- Their locations, including moves, with dates

- Their incomes and businesses or professions, including what positions they held

- Reproductive history including abortions, still-births and miscarriages

- Marriages and living-with arrangements

- Dates of births, deaths, marriages

- Highest degree in education, or year in school

All these facts are recorded on a family diagram (Figure 18)

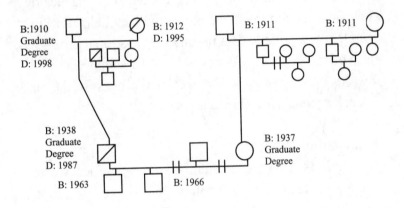

Figure 18 A Beginning Family Diagram

By convention, males are recorded as squares and females as circles. Some prefer hand drawing their family diagrams. Others prefer computer programs. There are several good software programs available to help with the project.

Bowen's goal, in making and researching the individuals on his own family diagram, was to get a one-to-one relationship with as many living people on it as possible and to learn as much as possible about other generations. Those who have followed him in that pursuit give rich testimony about its effects on their lives. They gain an ever-growing understanding of the "something much bigger than self of which one is a part," as well as one's own place in it.

Researching the Generations

How do people study their generations? One thing they often look for is themes.[2] Often people are motivated to study their generations with a particular topic in mind if they are experiencing a challenge or difficulty in that area. Some among many that have been researched are:

- **Death.** Different families approach the fact of the end of life differently. Sometimes family denial can reach amazing heights.

- **Survival.** Many whose generations were affected by the holocaust, famines or the Great Depression find that until they go back and learn all they can about the impact of that experience on the family, the anxiety continues to manifest itself in the generations. This may be so even though people don't know what the anxiety is about.

- **Reproduction.** This study, like many others, can remove roadblocks for a nuclear family experienceing challenges in this area.[3]

- **Money.** Different families have different attitudes about making, collecting, or the ability to earn money. Often these are rooted in past experiences of the generations.

- **Religion.** Experiences and beliefs of past generations can come down to the present intact, or they may be reacted to. This study becomes especially important when someone cuts off from the family because of religion or marries outside the family faith.

- **Divorce and Separation.** This study can be particularly useful when looking for family patterns of cutoff.

There is no end to the subjects that can be researched. And no end to the benefits gained in the effort. There is no better way to remove a "block" in life, work on a stubborn personality characteristic or irrational belief, or in general to become a little more objective, than to take a specific question back to one's generations, to see what can be learned from them.

Nodal Events and Watershed Events

It is important to look for "nodal events" – times when people entered or left the family. Nodal events can be tumultuous to the family – Bowen described the phenomenon. *"Death or a threatened death, is only one of many events that can disturb a family. A family unit is in functional equilibrium when it is calm and each member is functioning at reasonable efficiency for that period. The equilibrium of the unit is disturbed by either the addition of a new member or the loss of a member. The intensity of the emotional reaction is governed by the functioning level of emotional integration in the family at the time, or by the functional importance of the one who is added to the family or lost to the family. For instance, the birth of a child can disturb the emotional balance until the family members can realign themselves around the child. A grandparent who. . .comes to live in a home can change the family emotional balance for a long period. Losses that can disturb the family equilibrium are physical losses, such as a child who goes away to college or an adult child who marries and leaves the home. There are functional losses, such as a key family member who becomes incapacitated with a long-term illness or injury which prevents his doing the work on which the family depends. There are emotional losses, such as the absence of a light-hearted person who can lighten the mood in a family. A group that changes from light-heartedness to seriousness becomes a different kind of organism . . . A well-integrated family may show more overt reactiveness at the moment of change but adapt to it rather quickly. A less well-integrated family may show little reaction at the time and respond later with symptoms of physical illness, emotional illness, or social misbehavior.* "[4]

Watershed events such as immigration or the holocaust can have an effect for many generations to come and need to be understood as thoroughly as possible. People have often made long trips to try to understand better these events from living relatives in other countries who have knowledge about them.

Questions to Ask

Research questions, as in all good science, include:

- Who?
- What?
- Where?
- When?
- How?

"Why?" is not as useful a question to ask. It opens the way out of the facts and into people's interpretations of the facts, colored and reinvented by the emotional/feeling world.

Coaching

Traditional methods of psychotherapy pay little attention to the tremendous impact upon all of us of our generations. But the effort to understand one's heritage as fully as possible is one of the most beneficial efforts it is possible to make for self. It is a directive commonly given by Bowen theory oriented coaches and one already known in their personal experience.

The author's experience with researching subjects such as marriage, money and religion in her generations has left her with more objectivity in these areas and thus, greater ability to manage self in them.

Leadership

In organizations, the leader will want to know as much as possible about the factual history of the generations of a local group as well as any hierarchy, such as may apply in complex corporations or in a congregation. Here again, the seniors of the group become invaluable. They are a rich source of information. But they often give an added bonus. The process of sitting with them, listening to their stories and developing relationships with them can be a very stabilizing, grounding influence for the present leader, the same as it is in a family.

Often families or organizations, like individuals, get "stuck" after a nodal, or watershed event. In such instances a historical generational understanding can be immensely useful in getting past the roadblock.

Sometimes it is necessary to bring knowledge from one's research to the group in order to open up the issue and move past it. At times the seniors can figure in such a presentation, to their and the group's advantage. Or, a leader may do some enlightening research and then approach the group with what he or she has learned about the issue from the longitudinal approach. "This is what I have learned about our history. I wonder if it isn't playing a part here. This is how I think it may be working, and some options for ways that the issue could be approached. What do others think?"

Even if the leader is the only one to learn about historical issues, he or she will become a different kind of leader as the knowledge gleaned from this study plays its part in his or her continued thinking.

NOTES

[1] Bowen, M "Family Therapy in Clinical Practice" Aronson, New York NY 1978, 1983, 1985 pp. 384, 385.
[2] Dr. Anne McKnight has stressed the importance of looking for themes in family research over the years.
[3] Harrison, V Ch 10 "Reproduction and Emotional Cutoff" in *Emotional Cutoff,* ed. Titelman, Haworth.
Press Binghamton NY pp. 245-272.
[4] Bowen, M op cit pp.324, 325.

7

SIBLING POSITION

"We proceed from the assumption that a person's family represents the most influential context of his life, and that it exerts its influence more regularly, more exclusively, and earlier in a person's life than do any other life contexts."[1]

Walter Toman, 1962

Bowen's initial reading of Dr. Walter Toman's pivotal work, "Family Constellation" was a nodal event for the new theory. He instantly recognized the groundbreaking research as the missing component he had been looking for.[2] He welcomed it as another concept, "sibling position."

Toman said that his research was born out of a certain curiosity. Traditional psychoanalytic theory concerning human behavior said a lot about the parents' influence upon the children, but little or nothing about the influence of siblings upon each other. He thought it might be considerable. So he devoted his life to investigating what part the constellation of the family played in shaping personality and relationships. He interviewed literally thousands of families and individuals over time and in many different places.[3]

Personality theorists have long believed that much of personality is formed in the earliest years, out of experience in the family. It had been less clear what were the important factors in those early years. Toman's work identified the very order of one's birth, that of one's parents and the mix of genders among siblings as major determinants of personality characteristics, "all things being equal."

Toman often used the qualifying phrase, "all things being equal." By that he meant that many factors other than sibling position combine to influence personality so they may or may not be dominant in a given individual. But in the aggregate, statistically, the factors showed themselves to be important and significant.

The research showed that, all things being equal, people would show certain characteristics, depending on where they landed in their families' constellations, according to the mix of rank and genders there. He found that there is no sibling position that is better than the others. In fact, they all have their strengths and all have weaknesses. An oldest, for example, may be a natural leader, but will never have the sense of humor of a youngest.

The different positions make it quite clear that no two children experience the family in the same way. Each position is so different from any other that it is as if no two children have the same family. For example, the oldest can often remember a time when he or she was an only child and may be able to recall the births of the other siblings. The youngest, on the other hand, cannot remember a time when there was not someone older, "over" him or her.

Does the sibling position concept derive from the "family as an emotional unit" concept also? Even though it was discovered by another researcher, it is easy to see how all our patterned behaviors are developed out of the original family fusions we find ourselves in. In the same way, the "automatics" from our original family fusions we carry with us into adulthood will include those of sibling position. More fused families will be more affected by sibling position characteristics. Less fused families, less so.

There are eleven positions, all different from the others and each with its particular capabilities and vulnerabilities. This list shows each with its symbol following:

- Oldest brother of brothers b/(b)

- Youngest brother of brothers (b)/b

- Oldest brother of sisters b/(s)

- Youngest brother of sisters (s)/b

- Male only child

- Oldest sister of sisters s/(s)

- Youngest sister of sisters (s)/s

- Oldest sister of brothers s/(b)

- Youngest sister of brothers(b)/s

- Female only child

- Twins

There is no middle position listed. Middle children tend, often owing to age closeness, to be closer (to spend more time with) to one or another sibling. They will, as a result, adopt one of the above positions. Or they may carry characteristics of more than one position.

Here are short summaries of the "role portraits" that Toman found and described, condensed from his writing.

They are starting points for the important task of developing more basic self. They are not unchangeable and they are not necessarily applicable in individual cases. They do, however, hold true in the aggregate (statistically).

Oldest Brother of Brothers

- Assumes responsibility, authority easily
- Nurtures and cares for the group
- Expects loyalty and trust in return
- Sensitive and shy around women
- Attracted to youngest sisters
- Needs male friendships
- A concerned father if not controlling

Youngest Brother of Brothers

- Follows, leans on men
- Not a natural leader
- Interested in the quality of life and joys of the moment
- Accomplishes in scientific, technical or artistic fields
- Is soft, yielding, faithful, unpredictable with women
- Contact with males important
- Relates more as a companion to his children

Oldest Brother of Sisters

- Understands, appreciates, works well with women

- Not motivated to leadership, male chauvinism, male clubs, materialism or obsessive work

- Sacrifices for the woman in his life

- Concerned for his children but not overly so

- His wife the most important person in the family

Youngest Brother of Sisters

- Attracts services, care, solicitation of women.

- Charms women but does not understand them

- Valued and privileged in his original family and throughout life

- Can assume leadership easily

- Not keen for fatherhood, but indulges his wife's wishes

- Companion and advisor to his children

- Not interested in male friends

Male Only Child

- Prefers the company of older people throughout life, wanting their support

- Self confident and may rise to great heights

- Enjoys attention, life, art, intellectual and cultural exchanges, being the focus of attention, but not materialism

- Not motivated to fatherhood but may pamper and overprotect

- Father figures more important than male friends

Oldest Sister of Sisters

- Caretaker, order-giver, likes to be in charge

- Responsibility and power are more important than wealth and goods

- Intimidating to men, hard to give in

- Children more important than her husband, may be overprotective and smothering to them

- Women friends important

Youngest Sister of Sisters

- Bubbly, impulsive, loving change and excitement, attractive, competitive with other women.

- Works for recognition, praise, loves to excel

- Suggestible, can take risks

- Material things interest her

- Attracts men but may compete with them

- As a mother, may need help

Oldest Sister of Brothers

- Independent, strong, takes care of men

- Men in her life are main concern, does not compete with them, needs their companionship

- Would rather possess men than material things but can administer possessions well

- Loves caring for children, favors sons

- Less interest in women friends

Youngest Sister of Brothers

- Attractive to men: feminine, friendly, sympathetic, sensitive and tactful. Long-lasting relationships with men natural to her

- Motivated more by her man than by work or wealth

- Cared for by her husband

- Loving mother but may be dependent or seductive

- Women friends not interesting to her

Female Only Child

- Structures her life around older people and patrons

- Motivated by their approval and preference, not wealth

- Over close to mother

- Spoiled or egocentric with men

- Good, faithful wife

- Prefers being a child to having them

- Individual women friends preferred to groups

Twins

- Different from other positions in their closeness

- One senior, in charge and one dependent and impulsive

- Hard to imagine life without the other

- Relate to the other siblings in the family as from those positions also

Middle Siblings

- One role usually stronger but may have multiple roles

- May feel neglected in the family

- Relationship skills – may be known as the peacemaker

Sibling Position and Relationships

Predictably, different sibling positions relate in significant relationships in characteristic ways, all things being equal.

There are only two positions **without rank or sex conflict**:

- Oldest brother of sisters and youngest sister of brothers

- Youngest brother of sisters and oldest sister of brothers

Their relationships will tend to be those "fortunate fits." The youngest's tendency to follow will play to the oldest's tendency to lead. They each understand the opposite gender naturally, having spent a great deal of their formative years around it. These people seem to have to work at their relationship less. They encounter less problems in just getting along. They can't understand why the others have so much difficulty. Some of the reasons follow.

Four relationships have a **partial sex conflict**. That is, one of the pair has had no experience, growing up, with a sibling of the opposite sex. That one will need adult relationships of the same sex but the mate, not needing them, will not understand:

- Oldest brother of sisters and youngest sister of sisters

- Youngest brother of sisters and oldest sister of sisters

- Oldest brother of brothers and youngest sister of brothers

- Youngest brother of brothers and oldest sister of brothers

Though not completely free of conflict, one will understand the other better than vice versa but these relationships do not have the conflict of rank to deal with.

Four relationships contain **a rank or sex conflict**:

- Oldest brother of sisters and oldest sister of brothers
- Youngest brother of sisters and youngest sister of brothers
- Oldest brother of brothers and youngest sister of sisters
- Youngest brother of brothers and oldest sister of sisters

Though they have confluence in one area, gender or rank, they do not in the other.

Four relationships carry a **rank and partial sex conflict:**

- Oldest brother of sisters and oldest sister of sisters
- Youngest brother of sisters and youngest sister of sisters
- Oldest brother of brothers and oldest sister of brothers
- Youngest brother of brothers and youngest sister of brothers

Three relationships show a **complete rank and sex conflict:**

- Oldest brother of brothers and oldest sister of sisters
- Youngest brother of brothers and youngest sisters of sisters

• Only children

Relationships between people in these positions have less or no sibling experience with the opposite sex growing up, so they do not understand the other easily. Also, their ranks in their sibling configurations were the same. The oldests will be expecting the other to follow and may be shocked when it does not happen. The youngests will be looking for leadership that neither knows how to take. Though they may have a more difficult time of it, they can still have a stable and satisfying relationship though they may have to work at it.

Relationship Patterns and Sibling Position Combinations

What do we learn when we begin to think family systems about the sibling positions and relationships?

The particular flavor that relationship patterns take is especially influenced by the gender and rank of the participants in their family constellations.

Oldest children seem to be at risk for overfunctioning, just as youngests are for underfunctioning.

Often noticed by those working with families is the proneness of two oldests as spouses, to engage in conflict.

Youngests, rather than fight, will give in, so two youngests in a marriage will flounder, all things being equal, from lack of decision-making.

By the same token, marriages of a youngest and an oldest will tend towards overfunctioning/underfunctioning reciprocity, with the oldest in the dominant position and the youngest accommodating, of course.

Only children may be more distant in their relationships (need more "alone" time) than their mates are comfortable with. They may have to work harder than others to stay connected.

How Is It That All Things Are Not Equal?

How do all these fascinating and useful research findings fit in with the rest of Bowen family systems theory?

In the first place, as Bowen recognized from the very beginning, this information completes the theory. There would be a very large hole in Bowen theory without it. In addition, the theoretical and the research data mesh perfectly in some interesting ways.

Further, Toman often pointed out that his research applied statistically, or in the aggregate, but not necessarily in a particular case under study. Thus, his "all things being equal" phrase. How, then, do we account for the exceptions?

Things are rarely, if ever, equal. Because of the inequality of the family projection process, some people come out of their families more mature, or at a higher level of differentiation, than others. At the higher end of the scale, people will be less typical of their sibling position, with more of the strengths and fewer of its weaknesses. At the lower end, the opposite will be the case. They will be more likely to follow the portrait, or be "bound" by it. In this way, when the sibling position research is seen through the lens of the rest of Bowen theory we can begin to see why the research may or may not hold true in individual cases.

The sibling position descriptions are merely a starting point – one of many – for beginning the work on the self. It is differentiation of self that shows us how to work out of the weaknesses of sibling position, family generational history, or any other weakness we may find in ourselves. At the same time it teaches us about maximizing our strengths. Taken together, Bowen's and Toman's work round out a picture of human functioning we could have in no other way.

In Coaching

Therapists often read out of Toman's book to their clients, to reactions of astonishment: "How can someone who never met me describe me so perfectly?" This can open the door to new and energized effort. The sibling position information certainly takes one right back to the original family for answers to some of the questions we all have (or need to have) about ourselves.

For the coach, sibling position is one more piece of the puzzle in understanding the families that sit with us, as well as our own family relationships. It often takes the sting out of relationships that aren't going well, to realize "He is just acting like a youngest," or "I don't have to go toe to toe with this person just because he (she) and I both happen to be oldests." So the understanding of sibling positions becomes one more way of taking relationship glitches less personally.

It can be a great help for stuck relationship patterns, when sibling position does play a part, for people to understand how the positions tend to work together in relationship combinations.

In Organizations

People definitely bring the strengths and weaknesses of their sibling positions into their organizations. In addition, they can be pressured by the organization into a functioning position something very like a sibling position. Degrees, experience and qualifications may help bring one into the organization. But once there, the system acts emotionally as families do. The ones who have been there the longest often behave like the oldests in a family. The last-to-come may be treated more like youngests – told what to do, or treated as if they don't know much.

A very immature group can actually treat newcomers with cruelty. This is seen in the wild when young male primates migrate (in certain species where this is the norm) to a new group. At first the immigrant may be greeted with suspicion, rough play, or even violence. As human society has become more anxious, hazing of freshmen in various educational institutions has at times taken on criminal proportions.

A higher level group may treat newcomers better than that, even in anxious times, though prompting from the leadership may assist to bring about such a culture. For example, parishioners who are not welcoming to visitors are merely doing what they feel like (acting on emotion, not out of principle). In order for a group to grow, or even simply function better, however it may need some coaching on high level behavior. *Doing better (acting more out of basic self) is often counterintuitive.*

The fact that leadership most often comes easily to oldests and onlies does not mean that people in other sibling positions cannot learn to be high-functioning leaders.

On the contrary, differentiation of self shows the way out of this as well as any other relationship dilemma.

For all of us – therapists, leaders, parents or anyone else trying to improve functioning in relationships and in life – knowledge of sibling position is invaluable.

First, it improves functioning in one's own family relationships. As one understands one's own sibling position (as well as all the others) better, it opens the lens on the wonderful variation among people. This ushers in a new tolerance of oneself as well as everyone else in the family, with all their weaknesses and strengths, greatly assisting relationships with them.

As that takes place, there is a spillover effect in all the systems of which one is a part. The more one understands about how we all came to be the way we are, the less reactive one becomes to any particular trait. Parents become better parents. Coaches find themselves becoming more tolerant of others' patterns. Leaders are more effective leaders.

A knowledge of sibling position, used to understand and work on self, as well as to understand (and not work on) others, helps to remove one of the greatest roadblocks we all encounter in reaching for our goals – the relationship roadblock.

NOTES

[1] Toman, W "Family Constellation" third ed. Springer Publishing Co. New York, 1961, 1969, 1976 p. 5.

[2] Bowen's communications in the Special Postgraduate Program on several occasions between 1981 and 1987 made clear the historical process around these data becoming included as a formal concept of Bowen theory. Bowen and Toman stayed connected after that over many years as colleagues and friends.

[3] Toman's contribution to Bowen theory is extracted from "Family Constellation" Springer, New York, 1961 and from "Extraordinary Relationships," the text of which Toman read, edited and approved in 1991.

8

EMOTIONAL PROCESS IN SOCIETY

"There was growing evidence that the emotional problem in society was similar to the emotional problem in the family. The triangle exists in all relationships and that was a small clue. . . when a family is subjected to chronic, sustained anxiety, the family begins to lose contact with its intellectually determined principles and to resort more and more to emotionally determined decisions to allay the anxiety of the moment. The results of this process are symptoms and eventually regression to a lower level of functioning. . . the same process is evolving in society. . . we are in a period of increasing societal anxiety. . . society responds to this with emotionally determined decisions to allay the anxiety of the moment. . . this results in more band-aid legislation, which increases the problem; and that cycle keeps repeating, just as the family goes through similar cycles to the state we call emotional illness."[1]

Murray Bowen, 1975

Early on, there was evidence that as triangles in the family intensify, build and interlock, they eventually reach outside the family in networks that include agencies, institutions and friendship systems. In the 1960's the anxiety in society was increasing as order broke down in cities and universities. The family itself seemed to be breaking down as children ran away from home, hitchhiking across the country and adopting a drugged-out, irresponsible lifestyle.

Bowen responded by adding a new concept to Bowen theory, that of societal regression, as it was originally named. It stated that society is more or less anxious, orderly and organized at different times in history. In these times of societal regression, there is more anxiety in all people, firing chaos and irresponsible behavior. In turn, the chaos and irresponsibility create more anxiety, leading to more problems in society, in an escalating cycle.[2]

Many people seem to live in a state of denial about the existence or not, of societal regression, preferring not to think about disagreeable subjects. Bowen theory emphasizes the importance considering the facts before making judgments or taking action. So let's look at a few of the facts concerning the society in which we live.

Some Facts of Our Society

In 1940 the teachers in California were polled to find out what they considered the most troublesome problems they faced. The results were:

- Talking
- Chewing gum
- Making noise
- Running in the halls
- Getting out of line
- Wearing improper clothing
- Not putting paper in the wastebasket

Again in 1990, fifty years later, they were polled. This time the answers were quite different:

- Drug abuse
- Alcohol abuse
- Pregnancy
- Suicide
- Rape
- Robbery
- Assault

In fifty years our society had changed a great deal if the schools are any indication.[3]

Consider also that between 1963 and 1993 the crime rate went up 360%, youth crime is up 200%, teen pregnancy is up 600% and teen suicide is up 300% (now the second most important cause of death in teens, after accidents). One in five teens attempt suicide, single parents increased by 300%, SAT scores are down 7% and drug use is up over 1,000%.[4]

In 1991, less than 60% of children were living with their biological, married parents. Around 50% of children were living in single parent homes. There has been little or no change since then. Dissolution of the family is more the rule rather than the exception. 30% of U.S. babies are born out of wedlock. If a society is only as stable as its families, then our society is definitely in trouble.[5]

In 1999, Klaus Schmidt an intelligence officer of the European police force, Europol, said at an international conference, that the magnitude of the power and activity of organized crime is fast exceeding the ability of the police to address the problem in any meaningful way. He warned that organized crime could be in control of Europe in a short time.[6]

Regression in Nature

Regressive periods are not unknown in the non-human natural world.

Jane Goodall describes periods, among the chimps she observed, after fusion of two groups at Gombe when members of the group engaged in bloody fights among adult males.[7]

Frans deWaal saw disorderly conduct among the chimps he studied at Arnhem Zoo when the outcome of leadership challenges was in question.[8]

John Calhoun studied rats and mice at the National Institutes of Health. He noticed that when the population grew beyond a certain point, becoming crowded, there were many evidences of aberrant behavior. Mothers forgot how to make nests. Males gave up their nest "guarding" behavior and sat on the sidelines, staring (Calhoun named them the "barflies."). Homosexual behavior, unknown previously, occurred during the overcrowding periods.[9]

Roots of the Regression

What is at the base of the anxiety and ensuing societal regression in human societies?

Some that have been suggested include: overcrowding (especially in the cities), fear of annihilation by weapons of mass destruction, economic inequalities, economic ebbs and flows, loss of moral principles, diverse cultures trying to live together, technological advances overwhelming the senses, the media, the "Frankfurt School" with its avowed purpose to destroy Western culture, and ever-expanding government, making people less responsible for self and leading to over-taxation.

Another societal factor that has particularly interested the author is the possible role of the "helping" professions in adding to, if not instigating the societal regression.

The Helping Professions' Role

Ideas from the therapy profession have become popularized and have found their way into society as extremely strong forces.[10] There are many examples of how traditional theory regarding human behavior and societal regression coincide. Let us look briefly at only four.

- Permissiveness in childrearing
- The pleasure principle
- The sexual revolution
- Blaming of parents

The first is *"permissiveness" in child rearing*. The word permissive itself implies that parents are allowing children to do things they really do not want them to do. When this happens the children are in control of the family rather than the parents. Children are not ready and do not want to be in control of their families. Parents do not want them to be either. But fear of damaging children's psyches and the anti-authority trend of the therapy profession has left parents unsure and unable to take a leadership role in their children's families. This phenomenon drives anxiety up for everyone. As we have seen, when anxiety increases for more than the short term, a family can be on its way towards regression.

When permissiveness is espoused by society at large, as an ethos, judges, teachers, educators, the clergy – all who are in a leadership role – become unsure and unable to lead effectively. Their unsureness may become, for all practical purposes, irresponsibility. When the leadership of a society becomes unsure, irresponsible and unable to take a stand, the society is headed for, if not well into, regression.

Another regressive tenet of the therapy profession is that of the *"pleasure principle."* If one's main goal in life is to seek pleasure and avoid pain, then many other time-honored principles of emotionally mature living such as commitment, integrity, religious teachings and even the primacy of the family itself, fall by the wayside. It is not always easy or pleasurable, for the moment, to do what is best for the family, over the long term.

Making the right choice may sometimes involve some pain. However, if the pleasure principle is the main guiding principle of one's life, then if one's spouse does not bring one pleasure, discard him or her for one who does. This teaching, of course, wreaks havoc upon society's most basic institution, the family. As a matter of fact, however, eighty-six percent of unhappily married people who stay together find that five years later their marriages are happier. And three-quarters of people who have characterized their marriages as "very unhappy" but have nevertheless remained together report five years later that the same marriages are either "very happy" or "quite happy," meaning that permanent marital unhappiness is surprisingly rare among the couples who stick it out.[11] However, guided by the pleasure principle, therapists all too often have advocated dissolution of marriage if the partners did not seem "happy."

The *sexual revolution*, so destructive to the family and the lives of teenagers who entered into all kinds of sex prematurely, also had its roots in the therapy profession.

After all, Freud, the driving and shaping force of the therapy profession, based all development and motivational drives of the individual on sexuality. With his ideas of repressed sexuality, he paved the way for the fraudulent though extremely influential work of Kinsey in changing sexual mores. Kinsey, then, not content with perpetrating false data[12] on the profession and the public, went on to promote his particular brand of sex education in the schools – the "education" with an agenda – to legitimize every sexual orientation and behavior no matter how bizarre and unacceptable to emotionally mature, caring parents. Freud and Kinsey together have been, through the sexual revolution, an unbelievably powerful force in changing the sexual behavior and attitudes of Western society.

In addition, the therapy professions have been characterized by a tendency to *blame parents* for emotional ills of individuals. When people did not do well, or became symptomatic, somehow, parents were to blame. This was and continues to be, an extremely destructive force to families, putting parents on the defensive and leaving them confused and inept in their role as leaders of the family. When therapists begin to see the multigenerational process of which all of us are a part, however, it removes the blame factor and gives parents and others a way to understand a way of changing self in our families that is realistic and effective.

Regression and the Family

Has does the societal regression affect the family?

The family as an institution is not faring well in this time of regression in society. Neither are individual families. A few of the many ways the family is affected by societal regression are the following:

1. Societal mores have changed to an anti-family ethic.
2. Societal anxiety makes it more difficult to sustain relationships.
3. Rearing children is more difficult because of new dangers (sex, drugs, violence).
4. Two (full-time) career families stretch the family to nurture to the limit.
5. As irresponsibility becomes the norm, parents, like legislatures, take more and more short term measures, hoping the problem will go away.
6. The extended family is often far away (geographically and/or emotionally), not donating its important source of support for growing nuclear families.

In addition as the family is less a priority for society, corporations, the military, business and other organizations have moved nuclear families frequently. No thought has been given in our society to the importance of the extended family in supporting and assisting the nuclear family.

Cutoff as a Societal Issue

Even when outside forces do not separate the generations, families (not understanding the importance of continued connection), move away geographically or emotionally themselves from their extended families. Sometimes this takes place by isolating the older generation into "centers" and then not staying connected. The potential of cutoff in whatever form, for producing symptoms, is great.

As anxiety in society and thus in families, increases, cutoff can be expected to take place more often, adding to the problem that families face, both from increased anxiety attendant upon the cutoff and from the lack of resources a well-functioning extended family provides.

Because the society is more anxious, and anxiety is infective, families are more anxious.

Regression and Organizations

Does the regression affect organizations? The evidence is in every day's news that all the regressive tendencies so adversely affecting the family are also affecting all organizations, even churches.

Because of the higher degree of anxiety, relationships within organizations are more difficult, as people seem to "take it out on each other" and their leaders.

Chaos in organizations is illustrated by hostile buy-outs and take-overs. Organizations have overfunctioned buying many "perks" for employees and officers, then finding they cannot afford all these benefits, cut them off in a sudden cutback.

Large denominations that have been a mainstay of our culture are shrinking.

In the denominational hierarchy, officers are unsure what their role really is. Whereas the role of bishop used to be that of "the pastor's pastor," the author now often hears of bishops taking sides against the pastor, and with the anxious immaturity of local congregations.

Denominations are unsure of what they stand for, what they believe, or of their mission.

These same phenomena can be seen in all the organizations of our society.

Another Vicious Cycle

When the anxiety in a system increases, people tend to do more of what they have always done, (increase their togetherness, with all its patterns and postures) creating a vicious cycle. We have seen this phenomenon several times as we have examined the various concepts of Bowen theory

A regression that began in a relationship system can be resolved in a relationship system. In order to think at the simplest level about the regression in society, let us look again at the regressive emotional process in the human family, where Bowen first saw it.[13] Briefly described, when a family is subject to an overload of chronic stressful input, its anxiety level increases. It loses touch with its intellectually determined principles. Soon after that, one or more members are seen to develop symptoms. These can be physical, mental/emotional or social.

In the beginning a family may either ignore a symptom or do enough to merely relieve the immediate problem, then considering it to be solved. They continue as usual until another more serious symptom appears, followed by another superficial effort to relieve it. But the development of symptoms adds to the family's anxiety load. This then tends to increase the anxiety and then the number and/or severity of symptoms. A vicious cycle is initiated that perpetuates itself over time. The process repeats itself until a final "straw breaks the camel's back." One or more persons develops dramatic symptoms. This is seen as having developed unexpectedly. The end result is that the family regresses to a lower level of functioning.[14]

Resolution of a Family Regression

As we have examined the various concepts of Bowen theory, it is rather apparent that the way out of many of the dilemmas people face in their systems is for one person to calm his or her emotional reactiveness, start to think systems, and step out of the patterned positions (and thus the togetherness), taking a position based on principle. This is a step up for self, and as it turns out, for the whole system, for when one can go to a better level of functioning, significant others will follow. It is probably no less the case in society than in a family system.

For a family caught in the downward whirlpool of a regression, *one parent must eventually take a stand for higher and better functioning for self.* In Bowen theory this is called an "I position." It says, "I will no longer support irresponsible (dependent, symptomatic, regressive) behavior. This is what I believe (that everyone here is capable of better functioning). And this is what you can expect from me in the future." When this happens, others follow and the regression comes to an end. (Figure 19)

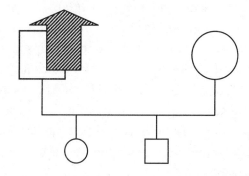

Figure 19 One Member Takes a Stand

Parents, Coaches and Leaders Can Make a Difference

Considering the magnitude and momentum of the regressive forces, is there any way that thinking, responsible people can make a difference? Of course, no one can tell anyone else specifically what to do in the face of the enormous tide of the societal regression in which we find ourselves. But family systems studies have taught us that people at any level of society have an influence on others around them. Parents influence their children. Friends influence friends. Spouses influence each other.

The greater the leadership responsibility, the greater the influence on society in general, of course. Societal leaders such as teachers, doctors, therapists, clergy, attorneys, judges, police and politicians influence a larger number of people in the wider society. For all of us, however, at whatever level of influence or leadership, a few principles suggest themselves in light of this discussion:

1. **Learn the *facts***, at some point, and begin to make a difference. *If societal regression is to turn around, people will have to get out of denial and start learning what is really taking place in society.* The truth helps us make sense of what is going on, take the chaos less personally. This will mean reading books and searching outside the usual media sources for facts. There is very little time on TV, for imparting the big picture – all the facts.

2. **Learn to *"think systems"*** in families and in organizations. Under the effects of heightened anxiety people tend not to see the "big picture"

or to "think systems." (Rather they tend to think "cause and effect," laying blame.) It requires work on oneself, but comes easier with time, practice, coaching, exposure to others who are making the same effort. If I know theory I can use it, if I don't, I can't.

3. **Get clear on one's guiding principles** and learn to think according to them rather than what society tries to dictate. If one believes the family to be important, for example, one will already be standing contrary to what much if not most of society dictates.

4. **Take a stand**, after careful consideration address the problems in accordance with principles. With clarity on the facts, and as much information on the process as possible, guided by one's best principles, a stand must eventually be taken. For a family caught in the downward whirlpool of a regression, *one parent must eventually take a stand for higher and better functioning for self.* Take an "I position," defining self clearly, calmly and in a way that can be heard.

Taking a Stand in Society

Do the same principles that help a family pull up and out of a regression apply in society? They certainly do in organizations, and there are many interesting examples of people who took stands and made a difference in their societies. Here are but a few:

A mayor in Poland recently said "No!" to a planned invasion of his town by regressive forces in the form of an illegal drug-based rally for teenagers – a "rave" – where the teens stayed high on "ecstasy" for over a week. He then organized the young people of the town to raise money for the local hospital. In interactions with the young people, the author noted that they seemed to be operating at a very high level of functioning – and seemed to be having a great deal of fun in the bargain!

There are other examples in history. In the Great Awakenings in England, where the Wesley brothers and Whitefield preached according to their principles of the Christian faith as they understood it, a societal regression, which had reached an abominable state, was reversed. [15]

John Adams, the second president of the United States, took many stands. His last was an unpopular decision not to go to war with France. It cost him re-election. But it saved the United States from going into an expensive war, having recently emerged from the Revolutionary War almost bankrupt. [16]

When Increase Mather, in early New England, learned the facts, taking a public stand regarding the Salem Witch Hunts, where young women were being imprisoned and executed, the trials came rather quickly to an end. [17]

In the U.S.-Iraq Abu Ghraib prison abuses, it only took one young man exposing them, to bring them to an end.

It would appear that many, if not all of the concepts in Bowen theory are so powerful *that if only one of them were adopted by a critical mass of people* (whatever number, or percentage that is) *it would make a huge difference to the society*. It might even start a trend that would reverse the regressive condition of society.

How many people would it take, *doing even one of the following* –

- Connecting with their generations, eradicating all their personal cutoffs
- Educating themselves as to the facts in our society – the regression
- Becoming clear on their guiding principles, being guided by them instead of political correctness or groupthink
- Taking a stand, after careful consideration
- Defining a self in their families
- Becoming principle-guided parents, rather than projecting a worried focus

– to bring the regression to an end? One can only guess how many it would take, but it is a fascinating question.

So, at some point, in accordance with one's principals, thinking systems about the facts and the process, one must take a stand. One person can make a huge difference, as we have seen. Writing, speaking and teaching as well as ordinary conversations become important in the stands waiting to be taken. There will be no changes in society unless and until we are able to know the facts, think about them in a broad way, according to principle and take a stand – or many stands – for societal progression. Perhaps for civilization itself.

NOTES

[1] Bowen, M "Family Therapy in Clinical Practice" Aronson, New York 1987 p. 386

[2] Gilbert, "Connecting With Our Children" John Wiley and Sons, New York, 1999, p. 15

[3] Ibid p. 12

[4] Connecting With Our Children, op. cit., pp. 11-14.

[5] Ibid

[6] Mut zur Ethik (Courage to Take a Moral Stand) Conference in Feldkirch, Austria, 1999, stated at the pre-conference meeting.

[7] Goodall's work described in deWaal, F "Peacemaking Among Primates" Harvard Press, Cambridge and London, 1989 p.71

[8] deWaal, F "Peacemaking Among Primates" Harvard Press, Cambridge and London, 1989 pp 69 and ff.

[9] Described in lectures given by Dr. Roberta Holt, who observed the Calhoun mice "universes" several times from 1981to present .

[10] Society has been enormously influenced by Freudian theory, through the therapy professions, though recent scholarship has shown psychoanalytic theory to be based upon unsubstantiated, misappropriated and false claims. See Crews, F "The Unauthorized Freud," Viking Press, 1998 for a summary presentation of some of the best of the many authors in this area.

[11].Bennett, William *The Broken Hearth* Doubleday, New York 2002 p. 158.

[12].Reisman, Judith, *Kinsey, Sex and Fraud, The Indoctrination of a People* Lochinvar-Huntington House 1990, p.117, 124

[13] Bowen, p. 269, 260

[14] Ibid. p. 273 and 386

[15]. Langford, T., Practical Divinity (Nashville, TN; Abingdon,), pp. 18, 19; Lane, T., *The Lion Book of Christian Thought* (Oxford, London; Lion Publishing Company, 1984), p. 168; Holifield, E. B., *Health and Medicine in the Methodist Tradition* (NY; Crossroad, 1986), pp. 3-4; Walker, Williston, *A History of the Christian Church* (NY; Scribner, 1970, 1970), pp. 454-470; and Williams, Jimmy "The Social and historical Impact of Christianity," www.probe.org/docs/soc-impact.html This site details the many societal reforms attendant upon the revivals in England and America and contains useful references.

[16] McCullough, D " John Adams" Simon and Schuster New York, 2001 Chapters 11 and 12, pp. 568 and 615

[17]. Reported by Dr. Roberta Holt, in a lecture to the Special Post Graduate Training Course, Georgetown Family Center, around 1990.

EPILOGUE

Taken together, the eight concepts of Bowen family systems theory form a coherent, cohesive elegant whole. In some ways the theory, like the family, is a unit. Some are more developed than others but there is no idea that is not needed, or could be pared away.

I hope it is clear by now how the concepts derive from that fundamental idea of *the family as the emotional unit*. They all depend on those family fusions of that relationship system we all grew up in. Out of that basic idea, proceed all the concepts in turn, even that of the scale of differentiation of self.

I had the interesting experience, in writing *Extraordinary Relationships*[1] of naively trying to write about only the concepts of the theory that applied to relationship functioning. But I found the concepts to be "sticky." In trying to write about one idea, the others came along too. They all interrelate, one to the other. They are all about relationships.

But it is not only the internal integrity of the ideas that validates them. Far more, the life experience of those who grapple with their understanding and use has shown them to be an accurate picture of the human experience. They should not be accepted blindly on faith. Rather, as one works for understanding and then experiments with them in life (with the valuable input of a coach who has been working with them longer) they show themselves for what they are. In this slow gradual way, they can become guiding principles for the basic self. There seems to be no way to rush the process.

They are a beginning, perhaps a stepping off place for further development of theory. For example, what about the development of a ninth concept? Bowen briefly thought about adding a ninth. He called it "The Supernatural." He did not continue the work, he said, because of the intense reactivity of the profession to it; and it never became a part of the formal family systems theory. Did he leave that for others of this and future generations?

Since Bowen's goal was to provide a theoretical framework that could eventually bring the study of the human into the realm of science, such a concept would have to be based on observation. Several people are intrigued by the challenge of such a ninth concept. One of the more noteworthy efforts is that of Father Joseph Carolin, who has hosted several conferences on the subject of the intersection between Bowen theory and theology.[2]

Additional work, interesting to me, is that of Koenig, McCullough and Larson. It is a "Handbook of Religion and Health" that includes summaries of thousands of studies found in the scientific literature on the relationship between religious belief and observation and health.[3] In general, the editors found a positive correlation. Even before the book was published, Dr. Larson had found that people who attend religious services are less prone to divorce, have more sexual satisfaction in marriage, have less delinquency in their children and less addiction.

His colleague, Dr. Dale Matthews, found that they had less high blood pressure, less liver disease and less alcoholism.

118

Dr. Joanne Bowen, an anthropologist, reports that there has been no culture studied that does not have a religious belief.[4] That fact alone would seem to argue for the inclusion of a concept about the supernatural or the religious phenomenon, in a comprehensive theory about the human.

Certainly, when thought through carefully (not simply accepted blindly) religious teaching can become (and has, for millions) a valuable part of the guidance system for basic self.

Whether or not a ninth concept ever becomes a formal part of theory, the eight do stand as a wonderful contribution to the understanding and further study of the human phenomenon. Further, they are a great gift to all who desire to try to do better in their personal life functioning. It is not unusual to hear those who have worked on self in this way exclaim, "Thank you, Dr. Bowen!"

There is much in this short book that is left unsaid. Many subjects are left to be explored – thinking systems, the coaching process, the nature of anxiety – each could be its own volume. A more in-depth understanding can only be gained by further reading, didactic courses, seminars and coaching with an experienced coach. The concepts themselves do not say much about thinking systems, seeing process, anxiety, or the coaching process itself. They do not draw direct applications to other situations than the family. Others are beginning that effort and I have tried to do a little of it here. In this book there are few examples. But the best applications are made and examples given, by the learner, himself or herself. Those are the ones that are remembered best.

Be warned – as you gain proficiency in knowing and applying the concepts, your fascination with them will grow, and increasingly, you will see their value. But this is no one-week study. It is not even a multi-year pursuit. It is a lifetime journey.

Because they are so useful and usable, it has been my goal to try to make the concepts of Bowen family systems theory as accessible as possible. Were they more a part of our culture, I cannot help but think our whole society would function better in many ways.

NOTES

[1] Gilbert, R Wiley and Sons New York.

[2] In recent years these meetings have been called "The Wisdom of the Ages" and have included a wide range of papers by some of the best of systems thinkers.

[3] Koenig, McCullough and Larson, "Handbook of Religion and Health" Oxford University Press Oxford, New York, 2001.

[4] Bowen, J (a daughter of Dr. Murray Bowen) in a lecture at the Bowen Center for the Study of the Family, Washington D.C., 2003.

THANKS. . .

. . .to Elaine Dunaway whose positive feedback inspired the frenzy of work that led to bringing this book into fruition,

. . .to Frank Giove, Mrs. Leroy Bowen, Joanne Bowen and Judy Bowen, whose reading, comments and appreciation now and over the years, gave energy and made this a better effort,

. . .to all those involved in the clergy seminars – participants, faculty and facilitators in Falls Church, Pensacola, Harrisonburg and many other places – where presentations and discussions of Bowen theory helped me to get clearer, especially Lucy Marsden Hottle, Carl Dickerson, Nicholas Lubelfeld, Scotty Hargrove, Kathleen Cauley, Bonnie Sobel, Jerry Foust, Tom Hay, Jacques Hadler, and Peggy Treadwell,

. . .to my original coach, Don Shoulberg,

. . .to the Bowen Center for the Study of the Family for being there through all the years of study and coaching when I was and still am trying to understand theory better, especially Kathleen Kerr and Roberta Holt, my coaches, and also, Michael Kerr, Dan Papero, Louise Rauseo, Priscilla Friesen, Victoria Harrison, Andrea Maloney Schara, Douglas Murphy, Kathleen Wiseman, Anne McKnight, Bea Flynn, Ted Beal, Mignonette Keller, Keo Miller, Marjorie Hottel, Regina Carrick, Patricia Comella, and Ruth Sagar, from each of whose thinking I have benefited,

. . .to Vail Mueller for her cover design with awe for her tremendous talent and to Jesse Mueller for keeping our computers working,

. . .to Elizabeth Foss and Kathleen Monge for their energetic assistance in research,

. . .and most especially to Joe Douglass, my loving husband, whose patient, untiring, enthusiastic and interested attitude and efforts towards computer glitches, editing, camera readying, finding and working with printers and logistics, as well as in understanding the theory, have been inspiring of themselves.

The Center for the Study of Human Systems
313 Park Avenue, Suite 308, Falls Church, VA, 22046

Founded by Dr. Gilbert in 1998, the Center's mission is to make the knowledge and benefits of Bowen family systems theory as widely available as possible. The Center disseminates information and organizes seminars and leadership training programs for parents, clergy, and organizational leaders.

Extraordinary Leadership Seminars are based on Bowen theory, which leads to improved individual functioning and leadership effectiveness in the important relationship systems of life.

Seminars meet one full day a month (October through June) over a three-year cycle. They are conducted by Dr. Gilbert and other experienced faculty members. For more information, visit our web site www.hsystems.org or contact the Center at 703-532-3823.